ERANOS
A Play

By Murray Stein and Henry Abramovitch

CHIRON PUBLICATIONS · ASHEVILLE, NORTH CAROLINA

www.ChironPublications.com

Interior and cover design by Danijela Mijailovic
Printed primarily in the United States of America.

ISBN 978-1-68503-558-7 paperback
ISBN 978-1-68503-559-4 hardcover
ISBN 978-1-68503-560-0 electronic
ISBN 978-1-68503-561-7 limited edition paperback
ISBN 978-1-68503-562-4 limited edition hardcover

Library of Congress Cataloging-in-Publication Data Pending

Table of Contents

Preface

"Eranos" is fundamentally a work of the imagination. It is a play. Nevertheless, it is based on a documented historical event, the Eranos Conference of 1947. The authors drew on many sources such as books, essays, letters, memoires, interviews, photographs, films, and other materials to portray the characters and their interactions. Some of the scenes make direct use of the original voice of the characters portrayed. While the authors relied on their imagination, they also kept in mind the factual material as known in historical documents. The "Eranos" in the play refers to both the Eranos Conference and to the magical setting in which Eranos is located, near Ascona, on the shore of Lago Maggiore. The physical setting of Eranos provides a key presence in the play, as though it were another actor, and its extraordinary effect is spoken of by members of the Ensemble.

This book is somewhat unusual in the history of drama texts in that it includes not only the actual script of the play but also chapters by members of the Ensemble (actors, musician, director, producer, playwrights) and others like Riccardo Bernardini, eminent scholar and Director of Eranos Foundation, and Dale Kushner, poet and novelist. Thus, not only are the voices of play's characters heard here but also those of the actors and indeed the entire production team as well. The characters in the play—Jung, Olga, Neumann, Rabbi Baeck, Aniela Jaffé—are fictional in one sense of the word, but they are based on well-known and much studied historical personalities. Readers may have to adjust their images of these figures as they work their way into the conversations being portrayed.

What the characters in the play are concerned about is largely the problem of evil and the enormous psychological and material task of recovery from the trauma of World War II. They are also looking forward to a new beginning. In fact, much rich work lies in the future for them. The play takes place at the end of one era and at the beginning of a new one.

Murray Stein and Henry Abramovitch

ERANOS

A Play

By Murray Stein and Henry Abramovitch

Characters in the Play

Olga Fröbe-Kapteyn—Founder of the annual Eranos Conferences

Prof. C.G. Jung—World-famous Swiss psychiatrist and founder of Analytical Psychology

Aniela Jaffé—Close friend of C.G. Jung and Editor of *Memories, Dreams, Reflections*

Erich Neumann—Jungian Analyst living in Tel Aviv

Rabbi Leo Baeck—Former Chief Rabbi of Germany and Concentration Camp Survivor

Narrator: Our play takes place at Eranos. Located near Ascona, Switzerland, on the shores of Lago Maggiore, Eranos was founded by a remarkable woman, Olga Fröbe-Kapteyn. The stillness of the grounds and the beauty of the lake and surrounding mountains create a magical aura. A large Round Table stands under the trees in the garden, and it is here, at the Round Table, where the play takes place. Near the Table, there is a stone with an inscription and two triangles.

It is Sunday night when the play begins, the eve of the Eranos Conference in August 1947. First you will meet Olga, then Jung who encouraged her to found Eranos in 1933; later Erich Neumann, Jung's brilliant disciple now living in Tel Aviv, and Aniela Jaffé, refugee from the Nazis, who under Jung's patronage became his personal secretary and confidante. Finally, we meet Jung's friend, Rabbi Leo Baeck, who had confronted him about antisemitism the year before.

This year's topic for Eranos is "Der Mensch," a German word impossible to translate simply into English. Perhaps "the Essential Human" best captures the meaning. Our play is not a traditional drama but rather a play about ideas and conversations concerning topics such as: "What is evil?" and "How does one recover from trauma?" The play is based on historical documents and testaments of the participants, but when necessary, we trusted the imagination to guide us.

As we begin ... Olga is in the Garden, alone.

Olga: (shaking three coins in her hands and tossing them on the table in front of her absent-mindedly while looking through a book. Suddenly, she stands, paces about and speaks out loud to herself)

What if nobody comes!

It nearly happened once before, in 1940. A dark night had descended over Europe, and only Heaven knew when we would gather here again. But I felt in my soul that nothing can extinguish the inner light. I asked Andreas Speiser, that lovely mathematician from Basel, to give a talk on Plato and the Trinity. Even if no one came, he would speak and I would listen, an Eranos for two. ... In the end, 40 people arrived. Even Jung ... and Emma. Eranos created a circle, a temenos, in which the work could proceed despite the evil raging all around.

(she looks into the darkness. Picks up the book again. Opens it. Puts it down and calls out) Is somebody there? (looks around anxiously) Is that you, Richard Wilhelm? Is that you, Wilhelm? You promised to teach me the Secret of the Golden Flower! You showed me how to use the I Ching. (raises up book) You inspired me ... to think about a life's project. ... My mother had no time for me. But my father ... Albertus ... In his eyes, there was nothing I couldn't do. After my husband died suddenly, father brought me here to Ascona, to the Monte Veritá Sanitorium for a health cure, just the two of us. Oh, I never wanted to leave.

After father's death, I went into seclusion. I studied the Vedas and the Upanishads, practiced yoga and meditation. I became so turned inward that I was in danger of losing my identity! I went to see Professor Jung, and he told me I had to change my attitude, to find an extraverted calling, to be more in the world. But how? I did a series of 200 vivid abstract and symbolic paintings ... and then... I knew! I would build an auditorium in the garden and hold themed conferences here. Again, I turned to Jung. He said,

"Make it a meeting place of East and West." Jung gave me the concept. And, that great student of religion, Rudolph Otto, gave me the name, Eranos—Greek for "banquet."

Here at the Round Table, we have a banquet of the spirit and the body, a place of encounter. Eranos is a mandala, a circle with many doors that lead to many fields of knowledge.

What if nobody comes?

(Jung appears and moves forward to the Round Table on the side of the stone)

Jung: Olga?

Olga: (coming out of her reverie) Oh, Professor Jung! Thank God you've come!

Jung: I came to look at the stone you have placed in the garden. (approaches the stone to the left of the Round Table)

Olga: It's the inscription you inspired!

Jung: (reading the inscription on the stone) *GENIO LOCI IGNOTO*: "To the Unknown Genius of the Place." (reflectively) I feel its presence!

Olga: See how the two triangles carved in the stone converge. ... One coming down from above, the other coming up from below. Together, they would form a six-pointed "star of David," the unity of heaven and earth. I feel energy from the stone. It gives me confidence.

Jung: (both sit down at the table) But, Olga, what are you doing out here in the dark and all alone?

Olga: I was just worrying if anyone will come this year. I even was beginning to consult the I Ching.

Jung: (taking the book in his hands) Enough worrying! Let's consult the Book. I see you have three coins. Throw them, and we'll see which hexagram emerges. Our question to the *I Ching* will be … (pauses as he thinks): "What is the hidden purpose of this year's Eranos gathering?"

Olga: (dramatically, she shakes the three coins in her hands and tosses them on the table six times, announcing the numbers as she counts them, each time in a new way. Jung is looking in the back of the book)

7 in the first place
8 in the second place
8 in the third place
8 in the fourth place
7 in the fifth place
8 in the sixth place.

Jung: It's Hexagram Number 3, Chun / Difficulty at the Beginning. What does Wilhelm write about this hexagram, Olga? (hands the book back to Olga)

Olga: (finding the hexagram and reading from the I Ching) Wilhelm says: The hexagram Chun connotes a blade of grass pushing up against an obstacle as it sprouts out of the earth—hence the meaning, "difficulty at the beginning." The lower trigram Chên means "Arousing"; its motion is upward, and its image is thunder. The upper trigram stands for "the Abysmal," the dangerous. Its motion is downward, and its image is rain. While the Abysmal sinks, a thunderstorm brings release from tension, and all things breathe freely again.

Jung: And the Judgment?

Olga: "Times of growth are beset with difficulties. They resemble a first birth." A first birth! What do you say to that, Professor Jung?

Jung: As you well know from the birth of your twin daughters, Olga, a first birth is beset by dangers. (silence for a brief moment. Olga, troubled, turns away or looks down, and Jung offers a simple gesture of comfort) Something new is emerging out of the womb of the unconscious. There is tension between the "the Abysmal" above and "the Arousing" below. I can feel the tension within myself.

Olga: Do you have any idea what it means?

Jung: We are recovering from a terrible period of trauma. The war is over, but recovery will be a long and difficult process. ... I have invited my student, Erich Neumann from Tel Aviv, to join us here. I haven't seen him in many years. He left Berlin in 1933 when Hitler came into power. He watched the devastation from Palestine. Not without great anguish, I am certain. He is just now emerging from years of isolation. But be prepared: His movement is upward and thunderous, like Chên, "the Arousing." When you meet him, you will see what I mean.

*****

Music

Scene II

Narrator: It is early Monday morning. Jung and Olga are enjoying the morning light. The Eranos Conference will begin later that afternoon. It is a moment of meeting between friends; a moment of looking forward but also of looking back.

Jung: (suddenly standing up from the Round Table as Neumann appears from the back of the stage) Neumann! (shaking hands) Please meet Olga Fröbe-Kapetyn, the Mother of Eranos. (all sit down)

Neumann: It's good to be back in Europe, but still disturbing. There are ghosts asking me why I would ever return to this place. My father was kicked to death on the streets of Berlin. I can't put that out of my mind.

Aniela: (coming to the Round Table, where she takes her seat next to Jung) I left Berlin in 1933 and will live in exile for the rest of my life.

Jung: What could be the meaning of the catastrophe we've experienced in this hellish War? People are saying we are now awakening from a nightmare, but nightmares are dreams, and dreams have meaning. What is the meaning of this evil we've experienced?

Aniela: It's clear that we desperately need a myth of meaning, a myth that would speak of the origin and meaning of evil itself!

Neumann: (thoughtfully) I too am wrestling with the problem of evil. You know, Professor, the biblical name "Israel" means "one who wrestles with God."

Jung: Struggling with the problem of evil is wrestling with God.

Neumann: All religions see the moral life as a wrestling match with evil. They believe that if humans try hard enough, they can overcome evil completely. They will be only good. But to be only good, they have to repress the shadow. But we know very well that repression does not eliminate the shadow. It gets projected onto scapegoats. In the case of the Nazis, it was projected onto Gypsies and Jews, homosexuals and the handicapped. I think we need a radical new ethic for the future, one that teaches individuals to take responsibility for the shadow and not repress and project it. The struggle between good and evil runs through the heart of every individual.

Jung: Olga, Dr. Neumann has just summarized his new book, *Depth Psychology and a New Ethic*. It's brilliant! He urges us to confront the shadow … within ourselves.

Neumann: Let me tell you what inspired me to write the New Ethics book. It was a dream:

I seemed to be commissioned to kill the apeman in the deep primal hole. As I approached him, he was hanging, by night, sleeping on the cross above the abyss, but his crooked, single eye was staring into the depths of this abyss. While it at first seemed that I was supposed to blind him, I all of a sudden grasped his "innocence," his dependence on the single eye of the godhead, a human eye, which was experiencing the depths through him. Then I sank down opposite this single eye, jumped into the abyss, but was caught by the godhead, which carried me on the "wings of his heart." After that, this single eye opposite the apeman closed, and it opened on my forehead.

Jung: Now you too can look down into the abyss! (long pensive pause) I, too, am tormented by the idea that there is an abyss of evil in the archetypal Self, that is to say, in God. Is God the ultimate source of the evil we suffer from in this world?

Olga: But hasn't God given us the freedom to choose between good and evil, even between *His* good and evil?

Jung: Perhaps. But often we are ignorant of what we are choosing. All of us are vulnerable to mistake evil for good and choose evil while feeling noble and justified.

Aniela: So, are we condemned to do evil and not know it?

Jung: Evil surrounds us. Our life becomes a battle between what we *are*—selfish, greedy, power-hungry creatures—and what we *should be*: generous, caring, open-hearted human beings! We are torn between the opposites within our nature as human beings. That is the real wrestling match.

Neumann: Let's talk about evil! A man sees a little girl drowning in a river. He starts to run to save her. But then he sees the way is muddy and his new suit will get dirty. He hesitates. The girl drowns. Is that evil? A second man sees a female mental patient staring into space. He says this girl's life is not worth living. He pulls out a knife and slits her throat. He feels like he has done a good deed. Is that evil? Another man sees mentally ill girls standing together, naked in a ravine. He says their lives are not worth living. He takes out a machine gun and kills them all. Is that more evil than the killing of a single girl?

Olga: I sent my handicapped daughter to a home in Germany where they said the care would be better. She was killed by the Nazis. Was I an evil mother?

*****

Music

Scene III

Narrator: It's Tuesday, Day Two of the Conference. The scholar of Greek mythology, Karl Kerényi, spoke on the topic, "Urmensch und Mysterium" ("Primal Man and Mystery"). And now, as Rabbi Baeck suddenly joins the group in the Garden, Jung's mind is flooded with memories of their dramatic meeting in Zurich just a year ago. He remembers Baeck's account of his years in Theresienstadt and also his own shame at realizing how the shadow came over him at that time.

Jung: (standing up from the table as Baeck approaches) Ah, Rabbi Baeck! So good to see you again. (they shake hands) Rabbi Baeck, our conversation in Zurich last year still echoes inside of me and has left a deep impression. I think often about how I slipped and went off the path in those confusing years before the war. I will never forget it.

Baeck: Our conversation brought back many haunting memories from my time in Theresienstadt, from those days when I was just a number, living like a horse, pulling a wagon of refuse in the mornings. Life I experienced in the gray zone. After our conversation, I realized that we *all* live in the gray zone. What that excruciating experience in the camp taught me most profoundly was to see every individual human being as precious and unique. My talk here is a direct result of our conversation. The Mishnah tells us that when humans stamp out coins, they are all identical; but when the Holy One mints souls, each one is unique. And more than that, God calls each of us to choose our own true path in life.

Neumann: (moves forward to the table) Rabbi Baeck, I have a question.

Jung: Rabbi Baeck, this is Dr. Erich Neumann from Tel Aviv.

Baeck: We knew each other in Berlin. (stands and bows formally in greeting. Then both sit down at the table)

Neumann: Rabbi, you emphasize the individual. Don't we Jews also live as part of a community? To be sure, I am not a practicing Jew, but I do feel solidarity with my people.

Baeck: Yes, for us Jews, life is first and last with our people. We live … and we die… together… as Jews. But there are times when a lonely man of faith must speak out—speak out against injustice. For evil to take over, it only requires that individuals remain silent. (silence)

Olga, there is a delicate matter I would like to discuss with you. … Recently, I received a letter from my friend Heinz Westman, who informed me that his Eranos lecture of 1936 was not published in the Eranos Annual Yearbook. Neither was Paul Tillich's lecture of that year. I understand that this was at the request of your German publisher who did not want anything in the book by Jews or by critics of the Reich. Did you speak up?

Olga: (tense pause) I was in a terrible dilemma. I felt if I spoke up and protested, Eranos would be destroyed. If I didn't, I would be collaborating with the Nazis. I had to choose. I remained silent. Did I go off the track? Did I?

(silence for a few moments)

Jung: The power of evil is pernicious and subtle. The Church, too, was often silent or complicit in what happened during those years when evil surrounded us. Just as I was myself. We *all* fell off the path.

Aniela: Can analysis deal with guilt and the problem of evil?

Neumann: Analysis can be very effective in relieving neurotic guilt when you feel guilty but have done nothing to deserve it. But analysis should not attempt to overcome actual guilt. However, it can start a process of returning. It can make the guilt conscious, perhaps illuminate it and point toward a *tikkun,* a repair, at the place where the human order was damaged.

Olga: The confrontation with guilt has a deeper purpose— to bring change in oneself, but…also in the family of nations.

Neumann: Confronting the shadow in oneself is essential for individuation. Our fascination with profoundly evil figures like Dostoevsky's Raskolnikov or Shakespeare's Iago reflects our hidden desire to know our dark side …

Jung: (interrupting) Evil is fascinating, I agree, Neumann, but only when seen from a safe distance, like on stage or in a novel. Up close … it is terrifying!

Neumann: But don't you also believe the light of the Self ultimately overcomes the darkness of shadow?

Baeck: In my tradition, we believe that evil occurs when the Holy One hides His Face.

Neumann: Christian theology considers evil to be the absence of good, "privatio boni."

Jung: Oh, Neumann, you know how much I hate the idea of evil as mere *privatio boni*. It obscures the reality of the power of evil. Evil lurks as an ever-present force in the world. To look away from evil or pretend it doesn't really exist as a power is dangerous. There can be no recovery from evil if you do not face it for what it is.

Neumann: The sad truth is that most evil is done by people who do not necessarily intend to do it. What happened to the Germans as a collective was that they were drawn into a mass psychology in which their sense of right and wrong was handed over to the Führer. Loyalty to the Führer became the definition of what was good; disloyalty to him was evil.

Baeck: Exactly! In these circumstances, the still small voice of the Holy One is drowned out and replaced by the masses crying out for conformity to the will of the Leader. The individual disappears in the mass. When I saw this happening to my countrymen in Germany … (lost for words) (silence for a time)

Jung: Yes! In this case, the mass psychology devours the individual. It is a man-eater. That is why I say that the collective psyche can induce evil in the masses; that is the source of evil. It is not absence; it is presence. (getting more excited) Don't tell me that evil is nothing but *privatio boni*! It has presence and it is powerful! It is like a pandemic driven by a wild and deadly virus.

*****

Music

Scene IV

Narrator: Wednesday evening. The Conference is halfway over. Today, Professor Gilles Quispel, Jung's Dutch friend lectured on Gnosticism, a topic that deeply resonated with Jung, which he will develop fully in his next major book, *Aion*. Quispel, in turn, will name ancient gnostic documents found in the Egyptian desert in Jung's honor as the Jung Codex. Jung and Aniela are sitting alone in the Garden Jung is somewhat exhausted. He is 72 years old, and has recently suffered two heart attacks. Aniela and Jung have a gentle intimacy.

Aniela: (quietly, musingly) I remember so well your spontaneous lecture here at Eranos not long after I escaped from the Nazis. It was in 1940. I took notes, and later together we made it into a beautiful essay. I'm thinking, maybe now it's time for you to speak … more personally …

Jung: (annoyed) No, Aniela, I have rejected the idea of writing an autobiography already many times. Autobiography is repugnant and ridiculous to me. I would only be misunderstood.

Aniela: I'm not thinking about an autobiography, but a story of your *inner* life. You could just talk to me. You taught me that these mysteries of the soul

must have a protection, a shelter in the room where
analysis takes place (pause). ...We could speak like
that. I would take down what you say, and then
I could weave it together into a narrative of your
memories, dreams and reflections. What do you say,
Professor Jung? Would you be willing to give it a try?

Jung: (a pause, then mildly) I resist, but on the other hand,
dear Aniela, to you I can speak freely. No one is quite
so intimately attuned to my thoughts and feelings
as you are. I must confess that recurring strong
memories of my early life have grown more frequent
with the passing years. Sometimes they explode into
my consciousness, and suddenly I'm taken back into
some emotional scene, especially into dreams I had
as a boy ...

Aniela ... dreams you had as a boy ...

Jung: ... I remember one so vividly to this day ...

Aniela: (taking up her pad and pen) Yes? Go on ...

Jung: I must have been three or four years old. I dreamt
I was in a meadow ... (he begins to reenter the
atmosphere of the dream in a reverie)

Aniela: (after a pause) Yes?

Jung: ... and there I discover a hole in the ground. I'm
curious and peer down into it. I can see stone steps
descending into the darkness below. Hesitantly and
with some fear, I go down the steps. At the bottom,
I find a doorway made of stone with a round arch
above it, the opening covered by a green curtain. I
push the curtain aside and see a mysterious dimly
lit underground chamber about ten meters long and

quite high. A red carpet runs from the entrance to a platform at the far end, and on the platform there is a fabulous golden throne. Something is standing upright on the throne. It reaches almost to the ceiling. At first, I think it is a tree trunk. Then I see it is made of skin and flesh, and on top of it there is something like a round head. At the crown of the head there is a single eye gazing steadily upward. The thing does not move, but I have the feeling that it might at any moment crawl off the throne like a worm and creep toward me. By now I am paralyzed with fear, and at that moment I hear my mother's voice cry out loudly: "Yes, just look at him! That is the man-eater!"

Aniela: The man-eater? What a terrifying experience!

Jung: Yes, exactly. I remember her words clearly. I woke up sweating and in a panic. For many nights afterwards, I was afraid to go to sleep because the image of the man-eater might return.

Aniela: What do you make of the dream? Was it related to a trauma?

Jung: Yes, definitely, to a traumatic experience I had around the same time. I was sitting alone, as usual, on the road in front of our parsonage house, playing in the sand. It was a hot summer day. From the house, you could see a stretch of road winding up into a forest. Looking up from my position close to the ground, I saw someone coming out of the woods and down along the road. As he slowly drew near, I could see that it was a man with a large broad hat and wearing a black robe that reached all the way down to his feet. I was terrified, and a frightening thought shot through my mind: "That is a Jesuit!"

Aniela: A Jesuit?

Jung: Yes! I had overheard my father speaking to a visiting pastor about the evil activities of the Jesuits in our country. I gathered that "Jesuit" meant something dangerous, something like a devil. Actually, I had no idea what a Jesuit was, but I was familiar with the word "Jesus" from the words my mother and I prayed to Lord Jesus every night before I went to sleep. Then we would sing: "If I die before I wake, I pray the Lord my soul to take," and this made me afraid of dying in the night. I thought to myself, "The man coming down the road must be the Lord Jesus coming to get me!" I ran wildly into the house and hid under a beam in the upmost hidden corner of the attic. I don't know how long I stayed there, but the hellish fear remained with me for days afterward and kept me in the house. And even when I began to play in the road again, the forest at the end of the road was still the object of my uneasy vigilance. Later I realized, of course, that the black figure was a Catholic priest.

Aniela: A Catholic Priest—the very shadow of the Swiss Reformed church!

Jung: Yes, the collective shadow—evil itself—was projected onto the Jesuits and the Catholics. I have tried to visit Rome many times, but I have never succeeded. On the rational level, this makes no sense, but for my unconscious, Rome is a most dangerous place. My inner child remains afraid of the Catholic priest. I have never really recovered. The priest was somehow akin to the man-eater in my mind.

Aniela: (cautiously) Was this your first experience of evil?!

Jung: Yes, Aniela. It's the first I can remember. The giant phallus was a symbol of a threatening god within the depths of the unconscious. It has blessed me with creative energy, but it has also plagued me with tasks and demands that often seemed beyond my capacity. It is a man-eater, definitely. The voice I heard—which sounded like my mother warning me of the danger—was speaking the truth: This spirit can devour you. I think of it as a second personality.

Aniela: A personality Number Two!

Jung: (nods in agreement) That's what I discovered at an early age. It has never left me. Called or not called, *It* is always present.

*****

Music

Scene V

Narrator: It's Thursday afternoon. Day Four of the Conference. Olga and Neumann are at the Round Table, which is covered with pictures and photos from Olga's unique archive.

Olga: Dr. Neumann, these are images of the Great Goddess that I have collected over the years. She is the woman with a thousand faces, the One who reveals herself in many forms.

Neumann: (looking intensely at the pictures, then speaking slowly in awe and with amazement) Extraordinary! When I look at these images of the paleolithic Venus, the pre-Colombian figures, the terra cotta goddesses from Crete—I see the Mother of us all—*She* who bore us at the beginning of time—the Mother of thunder and rivers, the Mother of trees and plants, the Mother of dance and song, the Mother of rains. She is the Great Mother of all things.

Olga: (with tone of reverence) The Great mother guides me.

Neumann: How did you come to know her?

Olga: Some years ago, when I was in Crete on a vacation, I was standing where the Snake Goddess was worshipped in the palace of Knossos. And I became psychologically entangled in this realm of ancient mythic figures and stories. The heat, the sun … I felt like I had a minotaur roaring inside me, I was spinning and faint. Then, I had the most powerful experience of my life. I was on an island beyond time, I was living in a sacred time … and then … I just dissolved and became the Great Mother. For a moment I lost my identity. I became one with Her.

Neumann: With the Great Mother Herself?

Olga: Yes. and I had another experience here at Eranos. On that small island in the lake—you can see it over there (pointing into the distance), not far away—there once was a temple dedicated to Venus. One evening as I was sitting in my room, I had a vision of priestesses coming this way from the island, walking in a long procession across the water and entering into Casa Gabriela. Again, I thought I was going mad. It was a vision. I made a drawing of it—see, here it is (showing Neumann her drawing)—another manifestation of the presence of the Goddess in my life. These experiences and symbols have become my religion. They have given me a light in the darkness, guidance and spiritual direction. I guess you would call me a pagan, Dr. Neumann. As a member of the Hebrew people, I suspect you disapprove of this type of religion. You worship a jealous, patriarchal God. I'm sure He does not approve of my worship of the Great Goddess.

Neumann: Whatever a jealous, patriarchal God may think about the Great Mother, I am in awe of Her. In my view, the Great Mother connects us to the Earth, which is the foundation of all. The ancient

Hebrew rituals and mitzvot do not speak to me. My Jewishness finds its expression in questioning, in studying texts deeply, and now also in living in the land of my fathers ... and mothers. The old ethic excluded those ancient goddesses, but today our task is to integrate the masculine and the feminine, not to split them. We must recover their essential unity.

Olga: For me, this is not easy. My early life was so completely dominated by my father. I loved him and worshipped his vision and energy. He was a force, believe me! My mother, on the other hand, was small and insignificant beside him. She was always in his shadow. So, when you speak of integrating masculine and feminine, I am at a loss. For me, it's one or the other. With these experiences of the Great Goddess, I've gone to the opposite. Maybe you can help me find a way to bring them together.

Neumann: You experience the masculine and the feminine in a power struggle. When there is love between them, you will find that they can come together.

Olga: (showing amazement) What you say conveys so much to me, Dr. Neumann. For me, images express my deepest experience. I am creating an archive of the images I have collected, and I want to publish them in a book, as a sort of comprehensive science of the soul. You are a man of eloquent words and able to put into language what I only sense and feel intuitively in the images. Would you be willing to write an Introduction for my book of images?

Neumann: (enthusiastically) It would be a privilege.

Olga: And next year, Dr. Neumann, will you give a lecture here at Eranos? Will you accept the invitation?

Neumann: Oh, Olga, yes. I say yes! I feel as if I have finally found a home ... here at Eranos.

(After the scene but before the music)

Narrator: From this stimulating and synchronistic encounter with Olga, Neumann's classic study, *The Great Mother: An Analysis of the Archetype,* is conceived and published in 1951. The English translation is presented to Jung on his 80th birthday a few years later (1955). Olga's archive would evolve and become ARAS: Archive of Archetypal Symbolism, a world treasure with images from every culture.

*****

Music

Scene VI

Narrator: It's Friday, and Baeck has just finished his lecture "Individuum Ineffabile." This is Jung's 15th visit to the Eranos Conferences. He had not missed a single one since its beginning in 1933. From conversations with Rabbi Baeck and others at the Round Table, Jung's controversial masterpiece, *Answer to Job,* will emerge.

Aniela: I found your lecture truly inspiring and healing, Rabbi Baeck.

Jung: But I was surprised by your lecture this morning. You experienced the full effect of the evil of Nazi Germany at Theresienstadt. I thought you would include the evil side of human nature in your talk.

Baeck: I choose not to dwell on the problem of evil, but to live ... to live with two sources of wonder: the starry skies above and the moral law within. For me, there is a grandeur in heavenly mystery, and in doing what is right, here on earth.

Jung: I want to pose a question that bears on trust in God. I agree that we need a new myth for our time, but it must be honest and all encompassing, given our recent experience. My question grows out of the Book of Job. This remarkable book contains an astonishing encounter between the Almighty and a human being, Job. My question is: What did Job learn when the   Lord revealed Himself? You will remember the dramatic scene in Chapter 38:

Jung: (stands)
Then the Lord, called out to Job from within the whirlwind.
(all stand as one)
Neumann: Who speaks dark nonsense?
Olga: Stand up now like a man.
Baeck: I will ask,
All together: And you will answer.
Aniela: Where were you when I founded the earth?
Neumann: Speak, if you know.
Olga: Who fixed the measurements of the earth, do you know?
Baeck: Who laid down the world's cornerstone?
Aniela: Have you been shown beyond the Gates of Death?
Neumann: Do you know when the antelope gives birth?
Olga: Who gave the wild ass his freedom?
Baeck: He Who argues with God.
All together: Let him answer.
(pause)
Jung: And Job answered the Lord and he said:
Aniela: (humbly) I am speechless: What can I answer?
Neumann: I put my hand on my mouth.

Olga: I have said too much already.

Baeck: I will speak no more. (pause)

Aniela: I knew You, but only through rumor.

Neumann: Now today, my eyes have seen You.

Olga: Therefore, I will be quiet,

Baeck: Comforted that I am dust.

(all sit down)

Jung: So I ask you: What did Job see with his own eyes—something … awesome, unexpected … overwhelming? And what did he learn? Are only justice and goodness found in God? Is not God responsible for Job's incredible suffering? What did Job realize about the Almighty in this astonishing vision?

(silence)

Aniela: Job saw God's reality, absolutely! Beyond good and evil.

Jung: Ah, Aniela. You understand.

Baeck: We must see Job first as a father, obsessed with imaginary sins of his ten children, constantly making sacrifices on their behalf. This sets the moral agenda: Who is guilty? And who must pay the price. Later, we meet Job as a father in grief, like a Holocaust survivor today. Consolation does not come from "friends," but only from Above. When Job does encounter the Divine Presence, he experiences something greater than he had ever imagined, and he is comforted … and blessed. Job discovers his place in the Universe and lives to see his great- great-grandchildren.

Jung: What about his earlier family? Does he not remember and mourn them? Will Israel not remember and mourn their lost children forever, Rabbi Baeck? (silence)

Olga: Dr. Neumann, do you have an answer to Job?

Neumann: For me, Olga, the key issue is how Job was changed by this experience. The final passages of the Book give the answer clearly. It states: Job had three more daughters. They were the most beautiful in the entire land. He gave them special names: Dove, Cinnamon, and Child of Beauty. And in an act revolutionary for his time, he gave them equal shares of his inheritance with their brothers. Job was changed, for now he valued the feminine and the masculine equally! That is a transformation.

Olga: But where is the Great Mother in this story? Is she just left behind, or left out?

Aniela: Oh, but there is Job's wife. Remember her! She expresses the Great Mother in despair. She has lost her children. For her, there is no consolation, no recovery, no transformation.

Olga: (weeping silently) Nothing can replace a lost child.

Jung: (after a pause) Satan, the dark shadow of God, walks the earth and creates unbearable loss and destruction. We must see Job as representative of our human condition. We are all subject to the harsh brunt of irrational evil forces. We may worship the Ultimate, but we must also fear it. It is ruthless. However, the Divine needs human consciousness to make It more self-aware, to become conscious of Its shadow.

This is what *the Almighty saw and learned* in His encounter with the man, Job.

Baeck: I agree that Job is representative of humanity and struggling with the meaning of suffering. God is beyond our comprehension. Job encounters this great Mystery as a lone individual. His vision is an encounter with the Holy Other as Thou. This is what Job saw, and it was a life-changing experience.

Aniela: (reflectively, as though to herself) A myth of meaning, if it is to address the problem of evil and heal the soul, must be grounded in the *mysterium tremendum*.

Baeck: Yes, the awe-inspiring mystery, as in the Book of Ezekiel, when God says: "Son of man, can these bones live?" and then says, "I will make breath enter you, and you shall live." We shall be like them, reborn from the dead.

Jung: Amen!

(Silence)

*****

Music

Narrator: It is Saturday evening. The Eranos conference has now concluded. All are seated, one last time, at the Round Table, before each begins the journey back home. But Olga has one last question.

Olga: For our last meal together at the Round Table, I have a request. I want to propose a question that is close to my heart: A question we have addressed many times, in many ways around this table. What is Heaven, and what is Hell? Can each of us share an image or an experience?

Jung: I like this proposal! I second it. Who will begin?

Aniela: (after a pause, thoughtfully) My story comes at the end of a great Indian Epic. The eldest brother of the Pandavas arrives at the Gates of Heaven with his devoted dog. The Guardian at the Gate says *he* may enter but *not* his dog. The eldest brother says the dog has been a faithful companion to him for many years, and he will not leave him behind. Later, he does enter heaven with his dog, but who does he see there but his evil cousins? He is shocked and asks, "Where are my brothers?" He is then taken below to a place of stench and suffering where he finds them. He says, "Wherever my brothers are is heaven," and decides to remain with them. So, I say: Heaven is where our "brothers" and our "sisters" are. Hell is where they are not.

Baeck: Frau Jaffé, your touching story reminds me of a Hasidic one. A pious Jew comes to his Rabbi and asks: "What is the difference between Heaven and Hell?" The Rabbi answers with a smile: "Actually, there is no difference. Both above and below, people sit at a great banquet table full of wonderful food, only their elbows are locked, so they cannot bring food to their mouths. The difference is that in Hell, people are starving, while in Heaven each person feeds his neighbor and is fed in return." That is the difference between Heaven and Hell.

Neumann: For me as a depth psychologist, our feeling of being in Hell, or in Heaven, derives from the quality of the mother-infant relationship. In the arms of the loving mother, the baby feels loved and so experiences "Heaven." In bitter moments of abandonment, the infant experiences "Hell." The torments of Hell— thirst, hopelessness, isolation—reflect the torments of the abandoned baby. We fear that place of despair, just as we long for the bliss in the arms of a loving mother.

Jung: As a doctor, I must say that my deepest experience of Hell was to watch helplessly as my patients have suffered the torture of insanity. Their endless screams and pathetic cries in the Clinic will never leave me. My hell was the feeling of utter helplessness in the face of their psychic pain and terror. My experience of Heaven was also in a hospital. While I was recovering from a heart attack a few years ago, I saw a vision of light where all my questions about life's mysteries were answered. I understood my life. My greatest joy has always been to understand, to know: *gnosis*. In that vision I got a glimpse of Heaven: to know even as I have been known by the One who has guided my destiny.

Aniela: Olga, you have not yet spoken.

Olga: (pause) My image of Hell is one I meet again and again in a recurring dream. In my dream, I am walking down a familiar street from childhood in the city where I was born. Then, suddenly, I realize I don't know where I am. In front of me is a locked door. I know I have the key, but I can't find it. I wake and don't know where I am. It takes me some time to realize I am in my own bed. For me, Hell is being locked out, alone. (pause)

Jung: And what of heaven, Olga? Tell us of heaven.

Olga: Heaven? (a pause) Heaven is being home here with you All.

*****

Music

Scene VIII

Narrator: It is again Sunday evening, and Jung and Olga are sitting at the Round Table.

Jung: Olga, do you know who first used the word "Eranos"?

Olga: No, who?

Jung: The Great Goddess of Wisdom.

Olga: Athene?

Jung: Exactly!

Olga: Tell me! Where?

Jung: In the First Book of Homer's Odyssey, that great epic of homecoming. (pause) But now it is time for …

Olga: … you to leave.

Jung: Yes … to leave. But I am worried about leaving you here and so alone at Eranos …

Olga: But I won't be alone.

Jung: (with surprise) Oh! Who is staying with you? Is it Aniela?

Olga: (laughing) No, not Aniela!

Jung: Not Aniela?

Olga: (she pulls out a ring and gives it to Jung) Read the inscription. What does it say?

Jung: (he looks inside the band and reads slowly) (pause) It says, "Love never fails," in Greek.

Olga: This is what I learned from you. If you are true to it, love will never fail.

Jung: True love remains … always true …

Olga: Finally … I am ready.

Olga: (putting on the ring and holding her finger high, she is radiant)

Jung: Olga, you look so happy!

Olga: Yes! Yes, I am more than happy. (pause, walks over to the stone) … As long as I live, Eranos, the Unknown Spirit of this place, and I will never be separated.

Narrator: And she never was. She created and recreated the inspired gathering at Eranos, year by year, until she died … in 1962. The spirit of Eranos lives on today … in us … beside a round table, by a lake, under the trees, waiting for the conversation to continue.

*****

Music
The End

Authors' Reflections on "Eranos"

A Dialogue Between Authors Murray Stein and Henry Abramovitch

Henry: Murray, it was your inspired idea to write a play about Eranos 1947 together. Why Eranos? Why 1947?

Murray: The notion for this play flowed directly from our previous collaboration on "The Analyst and the Rabbi." That meeting between Carl Jung and Rabbi Leo Baeck took place in Zurich in 1946. A year later they were together at the Eranos Conference, and the photograph of them seated together at the Round Table under the trees there has fascinated me ever since I learned who was seated there beside Jung. They look like old friends having a lively chat! What a transformation from the picture we have of them confronting each other just a year earlier. Our image of Jung continues to evolve as we collaborate on these plays. It is a real pleasure to work like this with you. I find "my Jung" constantly under scrutiny and in development as we engage.

When you think of an Eranos conference and imagine what it must have been like to sit at the Round Table and in the lecture hall, you soon realize there are many more people there than are shown in photographs. In the photograph of Jung and Baeck, we see only the two of them, but there were some 50 or more people present at the conference in 1947. Who were they? We learned that Erich Neumann attended Eranos for the first time in 1947. When we began to talk about that, things really started to cook!

Henry: Neumann and Eranos have been very important to me personally. My analytical training, which took place in Israel, was conducted very much in the shadow of Neumann. He would give advance versions of his Eranos lectures to his students, who were later my teachers. It was as if there was a spiritual descent from Jung to Neumann and on to his disciples like Dvora Kutchinski, who passed the tradition on to me and my companions. I also feel kinship with Neumann because of us both finding a home: his at Eranos, mine in Jerusalem. But it's strange that we wrote the whole play together and had it performed at the Jungian Odyssey in Davos, at the very hotel Thomas Mann based *The Magic Mountain*, and only afterwards did I visit Eranos for the first time. It was magical! When did you first visit Eranos, and what was it like for you?

Murray: That's quite a story. I first stepped into the magical grounds of Eranos when I was a student at the Jung Institute in Zurich in the early 1970s. At the time, Eranos was on every student's list of "must see" places. I loved it from the first moment. It was so secluded, a place to retreat to from the busy world of family and training programs. I wrote my thesis there over a period of several weeks. At the time, as it happened, James Hillman also was staying in an apartment at Eranos, writing his defining work in archetypal psychology, *Revisioning Psychology*. He was a fine chef and cooked us some wonderful meals. I remember roast duck in particular. So, when it came to working with you on the play, "Eranos," I could imagine the setting where the conversations take place vividly—the famous Round Table under the trees, the lake a few feet away, the *genius loci* stone to one side. It's amazing, Henry, that you visited Eranos for the first time only after we wrote the play!

Henry: Yes, I think your imagination led the way. When I did arrive, what struck me most was the profound simplicity of Eranos. It was not *in* nature but rather *part of* nature. You could reach out and touch the lake, or the trees, or see that dreamy island Olga refers to in the play. I felt like I was making a pilgrimage to the carved Stone and the Round Table, which feature so centrally in the play. I felt illuminated and thought of the last lines you speak as Narrator at the very end of play, how Eranos is both a place but also a state of mind, "waiting for the conversation to continue." I am not a person who likes the cult of personality, not of Jung, nor of Neumann. But I was so touched to be at the podium where these two Great Individuals stood and spoke and showed us so much. It was a moment of sanctity …

"What if nobody comes?" is the first line of the play. What does it say to you?

Murray: Olga is anxious. We had to imagine her reality—
the matron of Eranos, Olga Fröbe-Kapteyn, sitting
alone at Eranos for much of the year, planning for
the next conference, writing letters to the speakers,
planning for that one week in August when
everything had to come together. This gathering
of scholars was the meaning of her life! Our play
is set in 1947, just after the war's end. People were
still recovering from the horrific trauma of the total
war waged by Germany against the other European
countries. Switzerland had been isolated from the
rest of the world. Jung complained that he had not
been able to get his favorite British tobacco for
years! And now there was relative peace, a reprieve.
But the people were still far from back to normal
functioning. They were rebuilding their homes and
countries. Could Olga expect anyone to come to a
conference on world religions and psychology under
these conditions? She's not sure, she's on edge. That's
where the play begins. We want the play to reflect the
tense mood of the times. And we have Olga visioning
the presence of Richard Wilhelm while sitting in her
garden. Are we suggesting that she was psychically
unstable, Henry?

Henry: I don't think these usual categories apply to a
passionate, creative visionary like Olga. She never
met Richard Wilhelm, translator of the *I Ching*, in
person, but she did have several night encounters

with his presence in her own bedroom[1]. In another time, she might have been called "gifted" for her ability to receive spirits. It's also important to recognize her cumulating losses. Her musician husband was shot down during World War I trying out new reconnaissance technology behind enemy lines; the loss of her unexpected, damaged twin daughter at the hands of the German Nazis; and finally, the death of her beloved father who had inspired her to climb up Mont Blanc, alone, the hard way, and brought her to Monte Verità and given her the property of Eranos. Yet, I find her line, "What if nobody comes?" is also an archetypal expression of the universal fear of isolation and abandonment. I know this experience all too well when I am waiting for a friend on a street corner and feel the attack of Olga's question, "What if nobody comes?"

Murray: This is such an issue for our times, Henry. Loneliness and abandonment feelings are surging across the world. Our play is reassuring. Jung shows up in the first scene, then others come as well—Neumann and Baeck. Aniela is present, too, close by Jung's side. Olga is not alone after all. We have written of friendship, Henry. Our dialogue "Speaking of Friendship" tells the story of our friendship and reflects on how important this is in life. In "Eranos," we show the bonding of psyches in friendship. A solo

---

[1] See W. McGuire, *Bollingen*, p. 141.

performance at the beginning becomes a duet, then a quartet and finally a quintet—five personalities interacting and sharing their thoughts and feelings. It seems "Eranos" is about *communitas*, Henry. What do you think?

Henry: Yes, I do think it is about *communitas*. The conferences created a fellowship, which you and I came to feel part of while writing the play. Certainly, Eranos was a place of fellowship for Jung, and even more for Neumann, who came again and again after 1947, year after year, until he died in 1960 at the early age of 55. Olga liked to refer to Eranos as a dance. The dance continues even as the dancers change. In the play, she also says that Eranos is a mandala, a circle with many doors that lead to many fields of knowledge. Jung suggested that Eranos become a meeting place of East and West. Today, it's almost a cliché. But back then, it was cutting edge.

Murray: That's how I see it as well, Henry. The conversations that took place at the Round Table at Eranos following the papers in the lecture hall must have been especially challenging and pressing at the edges of the known. We have imagined Jung sitting there with Aniela at his side, Neumann and Rabbi Baeck nearby as well, and Olga presiding as the Great Mother hostess. And they are deep in thought and conversation about the issues of the day in the aftermath of the horrible war, and above all about the perennial problem of evil. This cuts deeply into the soil of the soul and prepares the ground for a new burst of creativity. It's amazing to see what follows from this gathering in 1947. Jung's late works— *Aion, Answer to Job,* "Synchronicity," *Mysterium Coniunctionis*—spring forth in the next decade. And Neumann's brilliant books break onto the scene in ways that astonish everyone—*The Origins and History of Consciousness, The Great Mother, Amor and Psyche,* and the bouquet of brilliant lectures from the podium of Eranos until his death in 1960. It's the emergence of this creative spirit that we aim to catch in the play. The unconscious is bubbling with energies waiting to be released by these characters.

Henry: This was certainly true for Neumann, who in a sense lived from one Eranos Conference to the next. There he found his intellectual and spiritual equals. In Israel, his disciples were so idealizing of him as a Great Man that none dared to make any comments, let alone a critique. At Eranos, he had "friends" who could both understand and challenge him. Baeck's lecture in 1947 was his only one, but he was crucial in getting the great student of Kabbalah, Gershlom Scholem, to come there, and once he came, he came again and again, 16 times. Scholem would always claim he was not a "Jungian," but he flourished in the stimulating atmosphere of Eranos.

The stone with its enigmatic inscription, *GENIO LOCI IGNOTO* ("To the Unknown Genius of the Place"), plays a crucial role at Eranos and in our play. I think the idea of "genius of the place" originally goes back to Roman religion.

Murray: The term *genius loci* meant the "protective spirit of the place" in Roman times. Jung gave it the added twist, *ignotio*, indicating the spirit to be "unknown," in other words a mystery. This is the spirit of the unconscious, which provided the inspired guidance for the Eranos Conferences. The topic for each conference was chosen by the speakers of the previous conference sitting at the Round Table and letting the *genio loci ignoto* speak to them and through them from the depths. This gave the Eranos Conference experience its magical atmosphere and quality. We refer to that in the play, especially in the opening scene. Wasn't this also how we wrote the play, Henry? Basically, we let the spirit of Eranos speak to us through these five imaginal characters.

Henry: We did let the spirit of Eranos speak. There was never a masterplan, nor an outline. One of us would begin to write a line, then the other would respond, and the unknown spirit would guide us onward, like water finding a way forward. At some point, we would meet on Skype and do a reading of what we had so far and see what worked, what needed revision, or even a new start. Implicitly, we each had a veto, yet trusted the other even at moments of disagreement. We were both working for the benefit of the Work. It also helped enormously that we were writing for the actors in the Ensemble. When we wrote lines for Olga, Jung, or Neumann, we knew who the actors would be. How did the idea of a Jungian Ensemble come to you, Murray?

Murray: We started with performances of collections of letters. When the correspondence between Jung and Victor White was published in 2007, to which I contributed as a consulting editor, I remembered performances of the *Freud-Jung Letters* that were staged by colleagues in Chicago. I asked my friends Paul Brutsche and John Hill to sit down with me and see if we could come up with a script for the *Jung-White Letters*. We had great fun putting that together. Paul was the perfect choice to play Jung because, among other qualities, he speaks English with the Basler accent, which was Jung's. And of course, John Hill, with his family background in Irish theater and Catholicism, claimed the role of Father Victor White with incredible verisimilitude and authority. This was the beginning of the ISAP ensemble. For the performances of "Scenes from The Red Book," we added Dariane Pictet, a fellow ISAP analyst and a trained actress, to play the several feminine parts. She brought the anima into the ensemble, and she has played those roles to perfection. This became the core of the ensemble. Our two plays (so far), "The Analyst and the Rabbi" and "Eranos," were built up with these actors in mind. For these plays, we included music at the beginning and conclusion and in the intervals between scenes, and we were so fortunate to find a professional cellist among our colleagues, Barbara Miller, who contributes the beautiful musical pieces that bring such depth and atmosphere to the productions. For "Eranos," we added two more

ISAP members to the ensemble, Kathrin Schaeppi and Gary Hayes. And you suggested we ask Michael Posnick to be a consultant for "Eranos." How did that occur to you, Henry?

Henry: Michael and I met at Yale. He was studying at the eminent School of Drama (Meryl Streep was there around that time). I was doing graduate work in psychology but with a passion for drama left over from my undergraduate days. Michael is an extraordinary person. On the one hand, he is a successful director who can tell actors what they must do, but on the other hand he is gentlest person I know. Soulful, spiritual, and with deep love of Jewish traditions, we connected deeply. Around that time, we did a number of unusual dramatic collaborations. I will just mention two. One was a dramatic presentation of "Zen Flesh, Zen Bones," Paul Rep's poetic evocation of Zen through stories and paradox. One scene made a very deep impression on me. On a blank stage, one actor comes on stage knocking, then banging vigorously, on an imaginary door, shouting, "Let me in!" Gradually, another actor comes to the other side of the imaginary door and starts screaming: "Let me out!" The second production was a script that I wrote and Michael directed, based on Martin Buber's writings, especially his exquisite *Autobiographical Fragments*, called *Meetings: Life and Teachings of Martin Mordechai Buber*. This play had a single but touching performance at a conference on Buber at the Yale Divinity School, from which you had recently graduated. Here, too, one line stays with me. On stage, the actor playing Buber gets an annoying phone call. Buber puts the phone down and says: "These rotten good-for-nothings... how I love them!" In the Ensemble, we had to be not only playwrights, but producers, stage managers, dramaturgists as well as directors. I thought that with the expanded Ensemble, it would be good to bring a professional eye in as a consultant and that Michael would be perfect. How was it for you working with him?

Murray: At first, I wasn't sure bringing another voice into our collaboration was a good idea. Would we lose control? He is a pro, and we are mere amateurs (I hope in the best sense of that word!). I guess I felt intimidated. That was before I met Michael. But as you say about him, he is most sensitive and kind, and I'm sure he was keenly aware of the potential for disruption. In no way did he ever try to assert his authority over us or play the role of superior expert. As it turned out, I found his suggestions to the Ensemble to be extremely helpful to them and to us as authors. His Notes were precise, respectfully delivered, and always useful. He is a lovely man, and I can see why you so easily reached out to him. I'm grateful for his willingness to participate so fully in our theatrical adventure! It was a minor miracle that his travel plans to Europe coincided with the performance of "Eranos" at Davos. From there you traveled with him and your wife to Ascona and paid your first visit to the Eranos grounds. What struck you most about that visit, looking back now in retrospect?

Henry: I want to first quote what my wife, Iva, wrote in a poetic mode:

Coming to Eranos was like unfolding an accordion-book, the experience got wider with time, and deeper in thought. Old stairs winding down towards Casa Eranos. Nothing is yet revealed, but the dense green, the blue water nearby, a balcony, and a distant statue in a niche. The house is impressive in its welcoming simplicity. Still—not telling, not revealing, but welcoming. Bringing in the serenity, the seclusion, the quietness. This is a place where one can think. One can look outside, and inside. One can breathe freely. This is the first impression. The first page. Eranos feels secluded. far from the touristic city of Ancona. But one has to go there—buy, eat, feel that other rhythm. Then returning to the parking place, opening the gate, winding down with the green, old stairs is more meaningful. I could feel the quietness engulfing me again. I opened one more fold. And the light of the evening, the sound of the water, the movement on the lake as darkness fell—that deepened it more. The next day we were shown Casa Gabriela. And there unfolded another chapter. The life of Olga, her vision, her tragedies, her energy. The beauty of it all. The depth of the need to have a dialogue. Maybe the thoughtfulness around Eranos, or maybe the ernest attempt to make it all work, and maybe the presence of all the knowledge – all of it made it deeper. Before WWII, a cable connected Eranos with Mt. Verita, connecting the spirit of the two places. The spirit of Verita—Truth, in its deep sense—is still there. The dense green, the water, the sound of light waves, and… freedom of thinking. That was Eranos.

Murray: That's beautiful, Henry. Iva is a poet!

Henry: In more ways than one. For me, what was most startling was to actually see the Round Table, made of a single massive stone, underneath overhanging eucalyptus trees. You and I had thought so much and talked so much about the Round Table, the setting of the play. But I was not prepared for what I encountered. The Round Table is a large yet intimate mandala. In our home in Montreal, we had a large round white table in the kitchen, which was the symbolic center of our home. These round tables give expression to the core values of intimacy, equality, and conversations ongoing, round and round. In the first scene, Jung and Olga decide to consult the *I Ching*. Can you say more about that?

Murray: Olga is anxious and has questions about what is to become of her big project, Eranos. "What if nobody comes?" she asks. It's at moments like this that Jung would have spontaneously reached for his copy of the

I Ching and some coins. That's what Jung would do with a patient in a circumstance like this, and Olga is his patient, in a sense. They are trying to understand the present moment and what it might augur for the future. I don't remember how we came up with that particular Hexagram, #3, Chun/ Difficulty at the Beginning. Do you remember if we actually threw coins and got that number? It does seem to work perfectly for the play.

Henry: It was my idea to introduce the *I Ching* because I sensed that this text unconsciously connected Olga to Wilhelm, and also to Jung. I am not knowledgeable about *I Ching*, but I searched the text for a Hexagram that would fit and found Hexagram # 3, Chun/ Difficulty at the Beginning. I felt that this Hexagram applied to Olga's difficulty at the beginning ("What if nobody comes?"), but it's also a principle in Classical Drama that a difficulty at the beginning must find a resolution by the play's end. In that sense, the final scene compliments the opening scene, because now Olga will never be alone.

Murray: A nice symmetry! One thing we discovered while writing the play was the much overlooked importance of Aniela Jaffé in Jung's later life. This discovery was made possible by the publication of Aniela Jaffé's book, *Reflections on the Life and Dreams of C.G. Jung,* which contains a historical commentary and brief biography about her by Elena Fishli. Aniela was always in the shadows, at Jung's side but not in the spotlight. In her own right, she was quite a prolific author, but there too she was hidden behind words about the Great Man. We have given her a central role in the play by devoting a whole scene to her effective persuasions to get Jung to speak his memories, dreams and reflections to her. And her repeated words about the need to find "a myth of meaning" for the times references her book with precisely that title. As it turns out, she was inspirational and a literary genius. She produced Jung's bestselling book, *Memories Dreams, Reflections*. Of the women around Jung, I would give her pride of place at his side.

Henry: I agree entirely. Aniela is the great hidden heroine of the International Jungian Movement, and Jung's *soror mystica* ("mystical sister"). Millions of people around the world know about Jung thanks to her unique gifts and dedication. In videos of Aniela, she can be seen smiling, empathic, a wise "young" old woman with pixielike energy. Her intellectual biography is also remarkable. Like Neumann, Aniela was born in Berlin. She entered at birth into a family of emancipated women. She studied medicine, specializing on feeding problems of infants, but turned to psychology, working closely with William Stern, the great pioneer of child psychology (who traveled with Freud and Jung to receive an honorary doctorate from Clark University and whose daughter-in-law was Hannah Arendt). She also studied under the great philosopher of symbolic forms, Ernst Cassirer, at the new University of Hamburg, and later with Jean Piaget in Geneva. In Zurich, she worked with disabled children and then in the children's ward of Burghölzli Klinik, where Jung had worked years before. She had planned to have a big family but had a miscarriage, which left her unable to have children. Rivkah Schärf, who years later was my teacher in Israel, brought her to Jung's seminars on children's dreams, and later she began a personal analysis with Jung. There was plenty of anti-Semitism in Switzerland, including in the Psychological Club which rejected her application for membership because of her Jewish heritage.[2] Later she became Jung's research assistant, the secretary for Psychology Club, and ultimately Jung's personal secretary. Robert Hinshaw, our close colleague who knew her very well, quotes her as saying: "I knew the path I wanted to take and took it, without shying from conflict."[3]

Murray: I totally agree with you about Aniela's contribution to Jung's legacy. She is an unsung heroine. In his conversations with her, Jung was able to show his vulnerable side as nowhere else in his writings or seminars. This endears him to us, and in the play it also endears us to her in gratitude.

We also lift Olga up into the spotlight for recognition. Her creation of the Eranos Conferences had a profound effect on Jung and indeed on a whole

---

[2] E. Fischli, "Historical Commentary," p. 241.
[3] Ibid., p. 373.

new discipline now called History of Religions, which Mircea Eliade, one of the many important figures to lecture at Eranos, brought to international recognition in his professorships in Paris and Chicago. Today, Olga's visibility is rising due to the work of Riccardo Bernardini, the Director of the Eranos Foundation, who is staging exhibitions of her paintings and writing about her life and inner development using her diaries ("Blue Books") and art-works. She is another unsung heroine, although previously quite well known as the creator of ARAS, the Archive for Research in Archetypal Symbolism.

Henry: In Hebrew, there is a special word for people like Olga, and it is "partizani." It refers to partisans working behind enemy lines in World War II, who are able to complete their unique mission, singlehandedly, against all opposition. Olga is such a pioneering "partizani" who was working from a strong "ego-Self" axis, serving the unknown spirit, not herself. Gershom Scholem wrote about Olga as a "living image of ... the Anima and Animus."[4] Significantly, she connects her own deep interest in archetypal images to the experience of seeing pictures gradually emerge during developing film in her father's darkroom. I deeply appreciate ARAS and make use of its resources often. Their masterful *Book of Symbols* has a special place in my office,

---

[4] G. Scholem, quoted in T. Hakl, *Eranos*, p 14.

lying on a bookshelf between me and my patients, so that symbolically we both have access to this direct descendant of Olga's collection. There were other historic events at Eranos 1947 that we left out of the play.

Murray: Yes, such as Father Victor White's presence there for his one and only Eranos lecture. Originally, we had planned a role for him, but the actor we had chosen to play the part declined, and we reconsidered his role. But Father White was a figure at Eranos and the Round Table in 1947. His relationship to Jung was, at that time, very strong and friendly. It would deteriorate in the years following, due to Jung's strong objection to the Catholic doctrine of evil as *privatio boni* and White's tenacious defense of the doctrine. In the play, we have Jung declare his hatred for that explanation of evil loud and clear. The problem of evil would be a central theme in his book *Answer to Job*, which would be published a few years later, in 1952. In the play, we find Jung getting ready for that brilliant outburst already in 1947.

Henry: Victor White was crucial for Jung. He stimulated Jung and was one of the very few who spent extended periods of time with him at Bollingen. White's lovely book, *God and the Unconscious*, is still a delight to read. Although they did have a serious falling out over *Answer to Job,* after Emma's death in 1955, they reconciled later, shortly before White's death in 1960.

Indeed, when asked who his true friends were, Jung replied, Victor White and Erich Neumann.[5]

There was another historic event that we did not find a way to work into the play, and that was the signing of the contracts for the publication of Jung's *Collected Works* in England and United States. Paul Mellon, whose late wife, Mary, had been a close supporter of Jung, came for the event and went on to provide crucial funding to Eranos and Olga, which allowed it to continue relatively financially secure until her death. He also provided funds, or travel scholarships, for participants like Erich Neumann, who would otherwise have been unable to come.

Murray: It was Mary Mellon who decided on the name for the foundation she and Paul would create for, among other works, the translation and publication of Jung's *Collected Works*: The Bollingen Foundation. Jung's Tower at Bollingen charmed her as much as the Eranos grounds. She and Paul visited Jung there in 1939, just before the beginning of World War II. The offer was made to translate and publish his works in English, and Jung agreed to the offer while they sat there on the terrace looking out to Lake Zurich. Jung was clearly thinking about his legacy, and Mary Mellon was a key person in that significant project. *The Collected Works*, translated by R.F.C. Hull and published by the Bollingen Foundation in

---

[5] A. Cunningham, "Victor White, A Memoir," p. 334.

cooperation with Princeton University Press and Routledge, would lay the foundation for Jung's legacy. But this project was postponed during the war and did not begin until 1947, when, as you say, a contract was signed at Eranos. Sadly, Mary had died in 1946 and could not see the result of her inspired vision.

Henry: Mary died young at age 44 from asthma. "I cannot breathe," remains a powerful phrase that continues to echo, literally and symbolically. I feel her loss even though she died before I was born. A key scene in the play is one in which all the characters discuss their idea of heaven and hell. What was the origin of this idea?

Murray: I'm not sure, but I really like the scene. It just seemed to pop up in our minds at the time. The stories are so varied and express something essential about the personalities and values of the speakers. When we think of heaven and hell, it's about the afterlife and legacy. What is Jung's legacy, Henry? I mean this in the highest sense of the word. What did he leave us that has value now and will have value in the future? This is, I'm sure, the question he is wrestling with. Hell is the absence of meaning; heaven is meaning for now and the future. What did he leave us with as a heritage?

Henry: You know, Murray, that would be a very good idea for a new play. We could call it "Bollingen" and conclude the cycle of plays we started with "The Analyst and the Rabbi." If I connect Jung's legacy to the Hasidic story Rabbi Baeck tells at the Round

Table, then it is one of attitude. We can make life a heaven or a hell for ourselves or others by whether there is solidarity or isolation, generosity or envy. More specifically, for me, I connect with Jung's idea that each of us has a destiny, which we can discover through the process of individuation. Also that we are more than we think we are. At times of mourning, there is a Jewish tradition to say, "May you have comfort from Above," which I understand as coming from the Self. What do you see as Jung's heritage for us today, Murray?

Murray: Jung's legacy is the stage he built for our plays, Henry! His work is so rich and multidimensional. To me, it's endlessly fascinating. My feeling is that we have not yet grasped the whole of it. And by saying, "Thank God, I'm Jung and not a Jungian!" Jung encouraged creativity and new developments. He did not create a finished system of psychology or philosophy, signed, sealed, and delivered. His legacy is that of a wealthy grandfather who leaves his fortune to his heirs and encourages them to use the resources he has provided for the good of all. Let's write about Jung's legacy, Henry. I like the title "Bollingen" for the next play in this cycle. Bravo!

A Meditation on Olga

By Dariane Pictet

Everything is ready, the kitchen is fully stocked, the cellar, too. Jung likes the Bondala Merlot she purchases at the little winery on the other side of the hills. Oranges were delivered this morning; they sit in their basket like prim balls of fire, atop each other in a loose pyramid, ready to be juiced for the ladies who will sit at the little table. *Why do I do this? I could have a simple life and paint all day.* She looks over the terrace at the hibiscus in flower and down to the lake to the island where she once had a vision of maidens walking across the water in their slender robes, heads veiled, lithe and graceful, bowing through the wrought iron gate, and into the house. *I wish it was all over, and they had all come and left, and silence could descend again on Villa Gabriella.*

I wonder if the housekeeper remembered to starch the white napkins for the lunch table. She sighs, so much to think about. *Every year it is the same thing, the invasion of laughter, the towering voices, the cars that come back and forth from the station until the guests settle in their rooms.* She glances at the drinks table, ready with jugs of lemonade laced with mint freshly picked from the kitchen garden. *I need the elements of wind, water, sunshine, and an exceptionally fertile earth to be present.* Her mind wanders back to her first years here, after her father gave her the house. *Otto Rank at Monte Verita with his naked ladies freed from the stifling corsets of Vienna's well-to-do society, prancing around the fields like children. Isadora Duncan was not the only one to dance in Ascona; Eranos too, is a dance, in which the performers change, but the movement continues. The Bohemian crowd was a bit wild to my taste, but they were seekers, in their own way. The peace that settled in after the first war was short-lived.*

So much sorrow when I lost my husband, Iwan. I can still hear his flute floating through our house in Berlin, notes rising, rising until they broke and tumbled down into an eerie silence. One night, the doorbell woke me, a telegram … my mind scrambled to make sense of the words … his plane crashed over the Alps. Now, now, no time for this.

She stiffens and crosses briskly the terrace, glances at the *I Ching* on the Round Table, and remembers preparing herself, aligning the wooden sticks, letting go of certainties to plunge into the timeless. Reading the hexagrams requires patience, the images must penetrate the silence. *Apart from painting, consulting the ancient oracle is what I love most. I hope Ritsema will be able to finish his translation … it must be made accessible to anyone who wants to mine the depth of this ancient wisdom, not just those who know the East well enough to understand Wilhelm's work. Only the uncertain path, the path with no guarantees, offers us the possibility of reading the signs … the uncertain path is the promising, the fertile, and at the same time the only path which remains open and receptive to truth.*

She closes the book, peers at the house, the cat leaps on the windowsill and settles there, paws outstretched. *The world is so dark ..., what a dreadful war, my baby, my little girl, so disabled, so clumsy. ... I feel so powerless, it's excruciating. I was so sure my daughter was safe in Germany. .... The Nazis.* She shudders. *Her spirit is free now, at least she does not suffer any more.* Tears well up again, and she brushes them away. Olga stretches her back, as if to claim back some structure in a body that always wanted to be water.

The blessing of yoga; the science of union, of bringing things together; Eastern tradition and Western gnosis. Yoga practice bridges soma and psyche, breathing deeply, feeling rusty limbs unfolding into a flow that stills the mind. The Gita taught me that when meditation is mastered, the mind is unwavering like the flame of a lamp in a windless place. But it needs to be mastered and mastered again. When anxiety befalls me, I forget and fall into Lethe, the river of forgetting.

It has been such a struggle to step out of myself, to open my house and my heart to all these people, year after year, for 10 days; the months of preparation, choosing the guests, sending invitations to potential scholars, refining the topics for the talks. And yet, so much inspiration, I can ponder the memories during the long winters, chewing them one by one until they reveal the central kernel, editing the papers for publication in the Yearbooks. Thanks to the Mellons and the Bollingen Foundation, they will endure.

The years seem to pass faster and faster: How long has it been since the first visit with father? Twenty years already? More. ... I needed years of concentrated discipline to survive the loss of my loved ones. The wisdom of the East held me together. I should breathe now, a deep in-breath. ... I just can't. I wish I could run back to my quiet little room, sit on the narrow wooden chair, feel the prickly woven coir against my shoulders, and let my eyes gaze out onto the lake until I fade into the stillness. If only I could be spared sitting at the Round Table, but Jung always insists and pulls a little stool for me to join the men.

She notices a butterfly fluttering on the lavender that spilled onto the steps leading to the lower veranda. *I like to see the guests, hear them, and be invisible. Yet, I also love wearing flowering robes, arranging necklaces, choosing the shoes that complement the outfit. Harmony settles me, there is a subtle order to things that brings beauty to the surface.* She remembers her years in Zurich at the School of Applied Arts, studying the structure behind intricate pleats, as she reveled in sewing, tailoring, and embroidery. She looks at the Round Table, a sturdy stone slab that took four men to carry up the narrow stairs and wishes she had placed it a little more to the left, *but it's too late now to think about that. I set the stage where the essence will unfold, the mandala, the circle in which the work can proceed.*

Olga was never comfortable with a rational outlook on life. Theosophy was her first love, bringing the invisible realm she sensed so clearly that little bit closer until she could step into the very vibration of the world. *At times,*

I can observe the anima flow into inanimate objects and lend a stone wall, a vibrant presence. My intuition was set free, shapes spilled out of me, yet it is arduous to put them down, to translate the visions clearly. It is such precise work, and so frustrating to see the multidimensional crystal forms land on the paper in a tight geometry that hardly reflected the scintillating diamonds floating across my inner eye. It is such a challenge to depict spiritual ideas visually, but I'm sure it can be done.

Jung hated my paintings, he told me to take them down from the foyer, I did, and that hurt. He called it the Devil's work; it was so harsh. I so wanted him to see and be elated with me by what sprung out of such deep inner spaces. He said they were cold ... if only he could see them waltz across my inner canvas. I wonder what stung him about my painted meditations. Maria Moltzer told him to devote himself to his art; maybe he feared that it would lead him away from psychology? It took me time and courage to lay my paints out again. Cold or not, I know now that I have to do it. Annie Besant understood this, and when she lectured on my Meditation canvases, she described the symbols as easily as some find their route on a map. Living with Alice Bailey was challenging. After she left, I distanced myself from theosophy. ... Jung entered and gave me a new direction.

Her eyes rest on the stone slab, where *"genio loci ignoto"* is carved ... "To the unknown spirit of the place." Here, giant peaks tower over a steel blue lake, rocks etched with dark shadowy pines that slowly soften into valleys and gardens. *Sometimes the breeze is so soft, it sings through the trees. Words have such power, she reflects, and so many words were spoken here. If I could paint them, they would be like serpentine flurries curling and uncurling in the wind. I did my best to preserve them in the Yearbooks, but images lead to transformation; our disease, our symptoms are unconscious symbols moving through the body.*

It was so powerful to paint my Vision series after using Jung's technique of active imagination. When I let the colors come to life on the paper, I know my soul is speaking. I step aside and feel the joy of not being me, guided by the invisible presence that creates through my awkward hand. And the surprise every time, when it tells me to stop, and I can see the finished piece and wonder at the Source of all things. I make myself small and let Her water flow ... Jung eventually wrote me that he had the impression that the figures were reminiscent of a sort of initiation into the Kingdom of the Great Mother, and he asked what an entrance into the cult of the goddess consisted of. As if I could explain it in other ways than through the images! They are my portal to Her who dwells beyond language.

Jung is bringing Erich Neumann here; he lives in Palestine, that land of stones and bones. Zionists want to create a state there. The map of the world changes like dunes blown by the wind, forming and reforming nations as if they were twigs that could settle anywhere. I was born in Denmark, spent my childhood in London, then moved to Germany; Munich, Berlin, Gersau, then to Zurich and now Ascona. I remember the terror that there would be no home to return to, each goodbye a wrenching, hands slipping down wet walls where no grip could be found. Then, slowly, the Great Mother nested inside in my heart, twigs became a hearth, a candle was lit, and when the world threatens, I take refuge there. I hope he will be interested in my images.

It was never easy to leave this house, but I had to, the images called. To locate them, I traveled across the lands, from Crete to America and so many places in between, they were buried in dusty archives, and I brought them home. She remembers crossly French librarians who hovered like demons over the books and manuscripts and became hostile when forced to hand them over. *I longed for a respite from logical thinking in words and concepts and fended them off with the magic wand of analogy. I needed to find the primeval ideas eternally existent in the psychic world. They have sought expression in every age and in every culture and are today alive and active as at the beginning of time.*

Father gave me the love of images. As a child, I sat quietly in the dark room in our London home while he developed his photographs. The white paper plunged in the revealing tray, shapes appearing by magic. We hung them with wooden pins, in neat rows, and they dripped on the stone floor until they were dry.

I wanted to catalog the motifs that appeared in dreams, to allow the dreamer to cross-reference their visions with images with as many different cultures as possible. They are an Eranos baby born in the darkest hour of European chaos. I could not rest until the phenomena of the unconscious in its various forms of written descriptions, phantasies, or drawings could be studied, compared, interpreted, ordered, or classified by competent workers in the field of psychology. But living with these images blurred the boundaries between myself and the great repository Jung calls the collective unconscious. Since archetypes do not require food or sleep, I, too, could not get proper rest and nourishment. I felt they needed to be assembled, sorted by themes, organized into a library of the soul, which brings inner landscapes to the world, to form a new history of Art, written from the standpoint of archetypal representation. This project took relentless energy and came from a deep sense of urgency. Collecting images is also part of my individuation process, like my paintings.

She reflects on the beginning of Eranos, and Rudolf Otto, more than a decade ago when they agreed that it should provide space for unbiased discussions about religions and mysticism; to conceptualize the feeling of the numinous at its highest level. *A sense of the sacred trails behind Otto. For him, the holy is wholly other, a tremendous mystery. For me, it is so intimate that it breaks my heart.* She remembers the first time the Great Mother entered her; waves after waves of love submerged her until she thought she would drown. *She poured Herself into my heart and broke it, again and again, until I disappeared into an immensity of love. All living beings were my children, I felt so proud of them, so moved by their presence that no judgment was conceivable, just joy and marvel at my courageous children, every one of them so unique, so beautiful. I held every creature that ever was and will be in a tight embrace. The experience lasted an eternity, and when it dissolved, something of Her remained, a trace of salt on my cheek.*

One year, Eliade talked about the illud tempus, *as a time beyond time, an eternal present that precedes thought and creation. That's how I feel when the visions come. Time is such a mystery. What is Being if not a clearing that reveals our original nature? I return to the Great Mother, to a source that is neither a time nor a place, the Alpha and the Omega. If only I could pierce the veil of illusion and see with my mind's eye what my heart already knows, then I could make one out of two, as when I am and am not the Great Mother. She laughs softly, I speak in symbols now, like Jung.*

I wanted Eranos to be a providential coming together of scholars who were intuitively moving in the same direction and open to the same ideas. Zimmer, too, wished to stay away from the spell of the logic of positivistic sciences and from those who remain unrelated to the content of the material they handle. Zimmer and Jung were instrumental in bringing the Great Mother into the Eranos discussions. Jung eventually thanked me for an abundant stimulus for the mind; what he called an exchange of thoughts with people of similar interests as well as the resonance from an educated audience.

They call me the mother of Eranos, and yet I only do Her work. The inward path is the only path to healing a world in chaos. The history of Eranos can be found in a book that has no writing, which I often go through, read, examine, and compare. I observe the images, too, in that there are many in this book, and I look for the connections that form the whole in a meaningful and unifying way. The overall image, the model that has become visible, is so wound around and interwoven with the model of my life that it is really hard to separate them. I am Eranos, and yet I don't know if I am. She laughs. *... Jung warned me about such identification.*

I hear a car ... they will be here any minute now. She feels her heart pounding and rearranges the soft pleats of her toga, the gold bracelets on her arms, glances swiftly at her reflection on the windowpane, shakes her head and walks assuredly towards the open gate.

Dariane Pictet,
September 2024.

About Being Aniela

by Kathrin Schaeppi

As we dressed up and practiced for "Eranos," I was often told by Paul, who had known Aniela Jaffé personally, that I looked like her—the character I was playing. When the play takes place (1947), Aniela is age 44, and Jung is 73. With their almost 30-year age difference, "Jung was impressed not just by the scientific background she had obtained with Stern and her in-depth cultural and philosophical understanding of symbols in mythology, religion and art, but also by her calm nature and maturity beyond her years."[6] This is a similar age difference between Paul (who plays Jung) and myself, and we share a similarly appreciative and respectful relationship as I imagine Jung and Aniela had, making it easy to take on our respective roles.

Early on, Murray and Henry had asked us to get to know the characters we were playing. I researched Aniela's biography written by Elena Fischli in *Reflections on the Life and Dreams of C.G. Jung* and was delighted to find that Jung said that Aniela early on in his experience of her had proven herself through a display of "psychological tact,

---

[6] Elena Fischli, "Historical Commentary: Biography of Aniela Jaffé," in Aniela Jaffé, Reflections on the Life and Dreams of C.G. Jung. Einsiedeln : Daimon Verlag, 2023, p. 238.

understanding and insight."[7] Oh, how I enjoyed slipping into those shoes!

There is an image of Aniela on the cover of *Reflections* that shows her sitting next to Jung beneath some trees— perhaps this picture was taken at Eranos—wearing a dark suit and a short string of pearls. She seems to be small-boned and rather delicate in stature, like me. Her dark hair is pinned up and pulled to one side. Her eyes are clear, direct, and kind.

I gained most of my insight into Aniela's character from the book mentioned above first published in German in 2021 as *Streiflichter zu Leben und Denken C.G. Jungs* by Aniela Jaffé's friend and literary executor, Dr. Robert Hinshaw. My admiration for and affinity to Aniela grew as I learned about how she navigated among the big stones thrown onto her path, dramatically changing its trajectory and taking her in unexpected directions. I also listened to recorded media and heard her humble, soft-spoken yet quite decisive and precise voice. She had no problem clarifying the interviewers' questions and then answering quietly with few words. So, with this in mind, it seemed appropriate that Aniela should add clarifying questions and sum up thoughts in the play.

Exile

Aniela appears in five of the play's eight acts. In Act 2, she says: "I left Berlin in 1933 and will live in exile for the

---

[7] Ibid., p. 247.

rest of my life." In Hamburg, she had written her dissertation and handed it in, but in 1933 her "doctor father," as one's dissertation adviser is called in German universities, was excluded from the University and consequently, without his presence, she could not receive her "doctor" title—ever. What a blow!

Aniela was quite aware of the building anti-Semitism in Germany, which culminated with her being thrown out of Hamburg University for not returning the Hitler salute. She subsequently had to flee her homeland and live exiled in Switzerland for the rest of her life. A paradox is that Aniela's mother had converted to Protestantism, and Aniela and her two sisters were baptized and educated as Protestants, yet it was their Jewish ancestry that determined their futures.

Aniela grew up in a reputable, well-to-do Furstenberg estate in Berlin. Her grandmother held a cultural and political salon and was emancipated for her time. Aniela seems also to have inherited the social conscience of her grandmother, who had cofinanced a mother-and-infant home in Berlin. At an early age, Aniela studied with the first woman to teach philosophy at a German University (Humbolt University, Berlin), Agnes von Zahn-Harnacki. She later studied medicine in Berlin and practiced at the Berlin Charité as an intern, working with children who refused nourishment. In 1929, at age 26, she married Jean Dreyfus, son of an art historian and an old Basler banker family. Shortly thereafter, as Aniela Dreyfus-Jaffé, she enrolled at Hamburg University in philosophy and the new area of child psychology. She studied with three of the most creative professors in Hamburg: William Stern, a pioneer in child psychology; Ernst Cassirer, a philosopher and author of *Philosophy of Symbolic Forms* (1928) and *The Philosophy of the Enlightenment* (1932); and Erwin Panofsky, a giant in art history. All three were forced to flee to the United States in the prelude to World War II. The play emphasizes how antisemitism affected both Aniela Jaffé's and Erich Neumann's lives.

It is noteworthy to mention that after leaving Germany, Aniela initially worked with Jean Piaget in Geneva. Her dissertation was not acknowledged at a Swiss University due to restrictions, though she received a job at the Clinic Balgrist in Zurich working with paralyzed children and then with psychiatrist Jakob Lutz in the children's division at the University Clinic Burghölzli for whom she edited a book on child psychiatry. She found desperately needed work in research, administration and secretarial jobs and in editing scientific texts for professors.

In 1936/37, during her free time she immersed herself in studying Jung's writings in the library of the Psychological Club in Zurich and went as a guest to her first Jung seminar at the ETH—*Children's Dreams*. Her soft eyes were indeed those of an analyst. She entered Jungian analysis with Liliane Frey-Rohn and in 1937 began to train with Jung once a week. Once recognized by Jung, she practiced as an analyst until her death in 1991.

In her life, Aniela showed a great deal of resilience and fortitude. In 1943, Toni Wolff, the president of the Psychological Club at the time, informed Aniela that she could not be granted membership in the Club, the reason given being that it was to protect Jung from attack by the Germans. Jung was outraged and demanded that the board reverse its decision, which it did in 1945. Seven years later, she became a member of the board! She was also instrumental in founding the C.G. Jung Institute, doing administration and secretarial work for its creation in 1948.

A Meaningful Coincidence

In Act 2 of the play, Aniela voices that humans need a myth to understand the meaning of evil, and she wonders whether humans are "condemned to do evil and not know it." She raises this question again in Act 3 where she ponders if analysis can "deal with guilt and the problem of evil." She speaks several times in the play of the need for a new myth of meaning.

This brought a sense of synchronicity in my life. In 2020, I was giving courses for Jungian students on Personal Myth and in 2021-22 had held a seminar over four semesters titled, "Finding One's Personal Myth," on discovering the meaning and purpose in personal and archetypal stories. In this connection, I had consulted Aniela's book, *The Myth of Meaning* (1970). Then, in 2022, I was invited to partake in Murray and Henry's play with its prominent theme of myth and the meaning of evil. My role as Aniela in the play seemed synchronistic!

Aniela and Jung

Act 4 of *Eranos* consists of a dialogue between Jung and Aniela. In 1955, Aniela became—with Emma Jung's blessing—Jung's personal secretary. Emma and Aniela had over time developed a mutual respect. Working with Jung, Aniela gradually became accustomed to Jung's expectations and his sporadically flaring temper. Aniela and Jung got along so well because their interests converged and Aniela's being extremely well-educated made her a companionable partner for the works they created together, such as Jung's essay on the Holy Trinity and *Memories, Dreams, Reflections*. She edited and commented on many of Jung's texts and was an accomplished author in her own right. It is lovely to read in Elena Fischli's biography of Aniela in *Reflections on the Life and Dreams of C.G. Jung* how much Jung admired and appreciated her work.

There had been much controversy about Jung possibly writing an autobiography, and Jung was in the mood to say no to it all. Scene 4 of the play enacts an evening at Eranos when Aniela encourages, perhaps even seduces, Jung into telling her some stories from his early life. (In real time, this type of conversation actually took place later, in 1956.) This scene imaginatively recreates their delicate collaboration in creating the memoir, *Memories, Dreams, Reflections*, which is, thanks to Aniela, a literary masterpiece that has aroused self-recognition in its readers worldwide.

In this act, Jung tells Aniela that he is not at all interested in writing an autobiography, and Aniela responds quietly that she is imagining a story of his *inner life*. Jung is won over by her charm and begins to recall a terrifying dream from childhood, and then adds an interpretation of what the dream meant to him. The scene ends with Jung drawing a portrait of his meeting Personality Number Two, a representation of the creative mind that can devour a person's life and carries the energy of a "man-eater."

I, too, have struggled with and had to confront Personality Number One (P1) as an empirical scientist and Personality Number Two (P2) as a creative writer and poet. Through personal experience, I know the confusing clash of the creative and scientific energies, the two souls that live in one body as Jung speaks of them. They plague one with their conflictual and oppositional energies; they battle and torment until they are accepted, reconciled, and integrated. This is an important personal and archetypal psychological insight raised by Jung and brought to life in this scene.

In real life and in the play, Aniela, while Jung speaks, takes notes in stenography, a type of shorthand in coded language that she invented for herself and perfected for just this purpose. This way she could quickly and precisely get Jung's words down at a time when Dictaphones were not yet available. I too learned the basics of stenography before transcription by Dictaphone became fashionable. *Memories, Dreams, Reflections* was largely recorded stenographically by Aniela, who then edited the text and published it after Jung's death (at his request).

No Consolation, No Recovery, No Transformation

Act 6 contains a discussion on the meaning of one of Jung's most controversial works, *Answer to Job*, a commentary on a biblical text. Aniela reminds the group that Job's wife had lost all her children. Speaking in her character, I say that for such a woman there is "no consolation, no recovery, no transformation." This is a heart-wrenching moment as Olga reveals that she had left a handicapped child of hers in a home in Germany, where the child was killed by the Nazis. She questions if she was evil.

Aniela knew already in 1932 after a miscarriage that she would remain childless. She was divorced from her husband, who wanted a family, in 1937. In reading *Answer to Job* and some of Jung's letters to Freud in 1952, she found that she appreciated "Jung's work in developing a psychology which did not shy away from acknowledging and confronting the dark side of the God image and the real existence of evil,"[8] as Elena Fischli summarizes her feelings. Jung's work "helped her to recognize, accept and bear her own sufferings ... as a necessary experience and part of the totality of existence."[9]

"What is Heaven and What Is Hell?"

In Act 7, all players convene at the Round Table at Eranos and begin contemplating the question: What is

---

[8] Ibid., p. 246.
[9] Ibid.

heaven, and what is hell? I have visited Eranos on its steep slopes that kiss Lago Maggiore. While there with a friend, we relaxed at the Round Table (then green) under the trees that cool in summer, and our conversations felt magical in the shadows of those who had gone before. Eranos is absolutely a *mysterium tremendum!* Olga Fröbe-Kapteyn created a memorable banquet rich in spiritual and ethical themes—a deeply needed compensation to the darkness of that time. Eranos continues to be a place for the coming together of people, sharing of knowledge, creativity and soul, for a greater good. The food shared at the Round Table symbolizes nurturing, caring, friendship. Olga's offering brought to life and honored the spirit of the Great Mother. It is indeed—in Murray's words—an experience of Self, with a capital "S."

At our retreats in Rougemont to rehearse the play, Darian opened her home and soul and created true banquets for us, much as I imagine Olga did with her guests at Eranos. This play, written by Murray and Henry and framed by Barbara's music and ensouled by each player—Paul, John, Gary, Darian and myself—and given depth and direction through Luis' film background and final podcast, and Michael's feedback, was a precious gift. The gift of play and friendship with exceptional colleagues. This indeed is heaven.

"I came to look at the stone you have placed in the garden"

On the Symbolic Significance of the Stone of Eranos

by Paul Brutsche

In his first appearance in this play, Jung greets Olga, who is deep in conversation with herself, in the garden of Eranos with the remark: "I came to look at the stone you have placed in the garden."

This shows Jung's particular interest in this stone, whose inscription *"Genio loci ignoto"* (to the Unknown Genius of the Place) he himself had inspired. The play makes no further comment on the significance of this stone, even though it is present throughout the play as a silent witness to a mysterious spirit. Since I was given the opportunity to make a replica of the real stone with suitable materials for the needs of the theater (see illustration), I would like to pursue in the following the open question of the symbolic meaning of this stone.

The Stone as a Visible Sign of an Effective Numen

In all cultures, stones have always had the purpose of representing something eternal and immutable, hence the custom of erecting a stone monument to famous people and great events. The stone that Jacob set in place at Bethel in the Old Testament[10] where he had his famous dream, as well as the stones that were placed on the graves of saints and heroes in the past, show the tendency to symbolize an eternal numinous experience with a stone. This is why in many religions the image of God, or the place of his earthly worship, was marked by a stone. It is well known that the largest sanctuary in Islam is a black stone in Mecca, the Kaaba. In the symbolism of the church, Christ was also regarded as a stone that was rejected by the builders, and the name Peter, which Jesus gave to his disciple with his blessing, means "stone."

Initially, this is probably also the meaning of the stone in the garden of Eranos. It is both a memorial and a monument to a *universal* spirit specially experienced in this place, which made it possible to ask fundamental questions about the nature of reality, human and divine.

---

[10] Genesis 28:18.

A particular feature of the spirit as experienced in this place may also have been that it was a *living* spirit that went beyond rational thinking and scientific argumentation, i.e., a transdisciplinary and experiential spirit guided by contemplation.

The stone also stands for an *objective* spirit, not in the sense of scientific objectivity, but in the sense of the objective substantiality of an inner reality. It is no coincidence that the theme of synchronicity, i.e., the correspondence of external and internal events through a factor of meaning that expresses itself simultaneously in things and in inner experience, was given special attention in Eranos.

Ultimately, the stone also stands for a *creative* spirit that, like the philosopher's stone in alchemy, enabled astonishing new insights and knowledge to emerge based on images and mythical tales. In this sense, the tower of Bollingen, built in stone by Jung, was also a special place of inspiration by a creative spirit materializing itself in a place and in stone.

The Meaning of the Inscription

Very unusually for a stone sculpture, the stone in the Garden of Eranos carries an inscription: *Genio Loci Ignoto*. In fact, the stone consists largely of this inscription itself. The stone is therefore less a sculpture than a place of remembrance, a memorial and a reference to a genius at work in this place.

The fact that language becomes a content and design element indicates that this place was primarily concerned with language and communication, i.e., with intersubjective understanding and cultural exchange, which was indeed a major concern of Eranos.

Moreover, the choice of Latin words could be understood symbolically as an indication of the universal approach Eranos was striving for, which pointed beyond the limited national, linguistic, and other particular perspectives represented by the speakers and listeners gathered there.

What is surprising about the wording itself is the fact that this stone commemorates a *genius loci* that is said to be "*ignoto.*" In other words, an "unknown" *genius loci* is being addressed. Why unknown? At a distance, this choice of words is reminiscent of the Tomb of the Unknown Soldier, which commemorates an anonymous soldier who fell on behalf of the many for a higher goal. In this respect, this *ignoto* has the meaning of an honoring commemoration of a hidden and human-related collective spirit. However, *ignoto* could also mean a mysterious genius and a spirit that is not officially recognized, i.e., a prescientific or nonscientific spirit as expressed in mysticism, meditation, imagination, and alchemical speculation. Eranos cultivated a "spontaneous speech of the soul instead of the language of psychology as a science," as James Hillman has written, whereby dreams, fantasies, myths, religions, scientific theories, the arts, and alchemy played a major role.[11]

---

[11] J. Hillman, "The Language of Psychology and the Speech of Soul," p. 299.

The Meaning of the Motif of the Two Triangles

The only figurative motifs on the stone are two triangular shapes placed on top of each other and touching at their apex. A slightly larger upper triangle is pointing downward, while a slightly smaller triangle at the bottom is striving upward. These two opposing movements characterize a dialectical pattern of thought in a formula like condensation that appears again and again in the play. It is a pattern of thought that characterizes the thinking practiced in the orbit of Eranos but is also typical of Jung's psychology. We first encounter this motif of a dialectical movement of opposites on a vertical axis in the I Ching, which Olga casts in the presence of Jung at the beginning of the play. When Olga asks what the hidden purpose of this year's Eranos gathering may be, she is given hexagram 3—Chun, Difficulty at the Beginning—in which the lower trigram, "the arousing," points upward, and the upper trigram, "the abysmal," points downward. The motif with the two triangles placed on top of each other is borrowed verbatim, so to speak, from the answer of the I Ching. The I Ching points to a tension, experienced by Jung in his own person, between an aspiring novelty that emerges from below from the womb of the unconscious and an upper consciousness focused on dominance, which is concerned with preserving the past and which, in this fixation, leads to abyss. Jung interprets the hexagram as a reference to the trauma caused by the war and the Nazis, which can only be healed little by little, or alternatively as the difficult birth of a new era.

Later, the motif of the conflict between above and below appears in the confrontation with the theme of evil. Neumann tells of a dream in which he jumps into the abyss of evil but is saved by the upper divine. Jung also speaks of such an abyss of evil, which is related to the upper archetypal self. The motif of the two superimposed triangles could thus also symbolize Jung's image of God, according to which the upper archetypal self, the creative God, has an archetypal counterforce, the abysmal evil, expressed in the lower triangle.

According to such a depiction, evil cannot be understood as *privatio boni*. Rather, it must be seen as a real existing downside to the bright upper triangle of God, as an independent lower antireality and at the same time a mirror image and alternative to the upper image of God. Of the same energy, but acting in different directions, of the same essence, the same completeness, the same autonomy, the same spirituality, as expressed symbolically in the two triangular forms, but at the same time each for itself and in inner opposition to the other side.

The central motif of a vertical contrast between the upper and lower worlds appears once again in Jung's childhood dream, which he recounts at Aniela Jaffé's insistence. In it, Jung descends into a subterranean room where he discovers a phallic underworld god, a chthonic daimon of creativity, whom Jung's mother describes in the dream as a man-eater. At this point, above and below take on the meaning of the upper, familiar world of consciousness in contrast to the uncanny, lower world of the underworld, or of a world of the conscious ego and a world of the unconscious shadow.

A further dimension of the contrast between the upper and lower triangle is later revealed in the contrast between the patriarchal and matriarchal spirit. In the conversation between Erich Neumann and Olga Kapteyn, an exchange takes place about the meaning of patriarchal and matriarchal consciousness as based on the contemplation of the pictures of the Great Mother, which Olga has collected and which Erich Neumann regards with great respect. Olga feels close to the Great Mother, who, in Neumann's words, "connects us to the Earth, which is the foundation of all. The old ethic excluded those ancient goddesses, but today our task is to integrate the masculine and the feminine, not to split them. We must recover their essential unity."

The Eranos motif of the two triangles can thus also be understood as an indication of the importance of a connection between an ethereal (upper) and a natural (lower) consciousness, between God and Goddess, between patriarchal and matriarchal, male and female worlds. This was the particular concern of Eranos, which manifested itself in the corresponding themes, but also in the corresponding thinking with a special sense for the reality of the imaginary. But the presence and work of Olga herself, the "Mother of Eranos," who once became identical with the Great Mother in a vision, was also of particular importance for the observation and appreciation of the matriarchal. She succeeded in bringing the spirit of Eranos to life in yoga with its intimate connection to the feminine, the world of images and spiritual body experiences. Not to be underestimated, also, is the importance of the location of Eranos itself, which, with its beautiful landscape and lush nature, helped to connect the airy spirit of the heights with the grounded spirit of the depths and to nourish not only the mind, but also the body and soul in the experience of a spiritual and physical feast.

Scene 6 deals with the confrontation between the tragic figure of Job and a Divine that is beyond good and evil. The conflict between the two forces, between the unpredictable Almighty in his absolute creative and destructive power on the one hand, and the suffering creature in his painful awareness on the other, can again be traced in the symbolic formula of the two triangles placed on top of each other. The upper, larger triangle pushes, as it were, from the open space of divine origin into the depths of human existence, where it meets the tip of an earthly individual, which is represented in the smaller triangle with a limited base.

The confrontation between the two unequal worlds, which is expressed in the motif of the two oppositely positioned triangles, contains a great potential for transformation. Job's experience of the boundless transcendence of the divine and his own limitations, i.e., the shattering of his human perspective, leads to an astonishing opening and expansion of his horizon: Job transforms himself into a father who not only has his sons in mind, as extensions of his own self as it were, but also his three daughters, to whom he bequeaths meaningful and cherished names and equal inheritances. The passage through a process of abundance, loss, powerlessness, and regifted blessing allows Job to discover the value of the feminine and the soul beyond his own ego fixation. The tragic destruction of the lower human Job in favor of the upper, the almighty Yahweh, leads to the realization of an equal coexistence of both worlds in the image of the Eranos motif: to a recognition of the masculine and feminine in their own dignity and essentiality in the sense of a balance between the upper and lower triangle.

The difference and correspondence between an upper and lower area, which is indicated in the motif of two triangles placed on top of each other and which characterizes the creatively bipolar and integrative spirit of Eranos, is expressed in the play, as shown, in various places and in various forms. Here is another and final form. At the last meal together at the end of the Eranos meeting, Olga suggests a theme very close to her heart and on which everyone present is asked to comment. What is heaven, and what is hell? Everyone is invited to contribute with a picture or an experience. This theme obviously fits into the framework of a vertical juxtaposition of an upper and lower, a light and dark, a positive and negative, a patriarchal and matriarchal, a male and female world, which is part of the essence of the view practiced at Eranos. This opposition of two levels was never about a dualistic devaluation of one level, but about the integration of both into a more complete view of things. This integrative and complex approach corresponded to the spirit of Eranos, just as it determined the basic attitude of the guiding participant C.G. Jung, whose psychology was once called "complex psychology" for good reason.

The answers given by the various participants about heaven and hell are based on different experiences and images, but nevertheless they have something in common: "Heaven" is associated with the experience of community and "Hell" with the experience of isolation and loneliness.[12] With these answers drawn from personal experience, each participant contributes something to the banquet. They are mental souvenirs for the communal picnic, and this was in fact the original meaning of the word Eranos.

It is significant that toward the end of the play, the transcendent, "heavenly" value of community is pointed out and that the word Eranos is thus emphasized in its communal and identity-forming meaning.

The Stone in Different Contexts: The Multiple Relational Dimensions of the *Genius Loci*

Regarding the symbolic meaning of the stone at Eranos, there are four aspects to consider: its relationship to the place Moscia in Ticino; its proximity to the Round Table in Eranos; its reference to the dimension of time and

---

[12] Aniela: "Heaven is where our 'brothers' and our 'sisters' are. Hell is where they are not." Baeck: "In Hell, people are starving, while in Heaven each person feeds his neighbor and is fed in return." Neumann: "In the arms of the loving mother, the baby feels loved and so experiences 'Heaven.' In bitter moments of abandonment, the infant experiences 'Hell.'" Jung: "My hell was the feeling of utter helplessness in the face of the psychic pain and terror of my patients who suffered the torture of insanity. Heaven: to know even as I have been known by the One who has guided my destiny." Olga: "Hell is being locked out, alone. Heaven is being home here, with you all."

the historical moment; and finally Olga's relationship to the symbolic stone and its meaning.

First, on the placement of the stone in Moscia, in Ticino: The fact that the stone stands in the garden of Eranos in the immediate vicinity of Lake Maggiore, which geographically connects the Italian regions of Piedmont and Lombardy with Switzerland, and at the same time in the immediate vicinity of Monte Verità, where experiments for new forms of life and liberated selfhood were carried out at the beginning of the 20th century,[13] is significant. It is an area of connection and cultural exchange between south and north, Mediterranean culture and the transalpine mind. And it is an area of revolutionary innovation and the invention of a "true" way of life[14] without the constraints of tradition and institution. The stone stands in a place where many creative contemporaries felt magically drawn, where the Zeitgeist was questioned and new ways of life were tried out in a reflection on nature, and where there was thus a certain affinity with the spirit who lived in Eranos. This place had a special aura; it had a renewing, creative and healing effect. Olga had regained her health here in the sanatorium on Monte Verità. That was the extended *genus loci* of this area so open to renewal.

---

[13] Which included a new philosophy of life, a return to nature, liberation from all shackles, a vegetarian diet, exercise in the great outdoors, sunbathing, nudism and theosophy) and where seekers, cultural workers, artists, analysts and anarchists from Germany, Austria, Russia and Switzerland, among others, came together.

[14] Therefore, Monte Verità.

Second, the location of the stone in the immediate vicinity of the Round Table where the conversations took place. The proximity to the table made it clear that the two belonged together: a stelelike witness to a mysterious spirit and the exchange of thoughts in the open community of participants. Just as in a Catholic church Christ is seen as present in the form of the Host kept in the tabernacle and at the same time is made present anew in the celebration of Mass by the community, there is a reciprocal relationship between the stone and the Eranos community. The spirit of creative knowledge symbolically witnessed in the stone is brought to life anew in the conversations of the community. And conversely, the conversations in the community bring the numinosity of the stone to life, i.e., they promote the certainty of being on the trail of an ultimately incomprehensible creative force that reveals and conceals itself and ultimately enables and produces all knowledge.

Third, on the relationship of the stone to the dimension of time and to the historical moment. The stone itself seems to point to a dimension of time insofar as the previously discussed motif of the two triangles placed on top of each other can also be seen as a geometric depiction of an hourglass. In this sense, the symbolic statement would be that the *genius loci* is present here and now and that it always works within the horizon of time and impacts on the particular moment. The stone testifies to the presence of a spirit that appears at this precise moment and is necessary and probably only possible now. When Olga asks Jung at the beginning of the play how he understands the *I Ching* hexagram Chun: Difficulty at the Beginning, he refers to the contemporary historical situation: "We are recovering from a terrible period of trauma. The war is over, but recovery will be a long and difficult process." The hidden genius of the place, which is witnessed in the stone of Eranos, is thus analogous to the general situation of the times, which is characterized by the trauma of war, but also by painful new beginnings.

Fourth, the significance of the stone for Olga's relationship to Eranos. In the final scene of the play, Olga makes contact with the stone, just as Jung expressed his interest in it at the beginning. The stone thus frames the entire play and at the same time is present as a counterpart for the entire duration. The stone gives Olga the certainty that she is forever connected to Eranos, the unknown spirit of this place. Insofar as the stone embodies, objectifies, and visualizes this spirit in the truest sense, Olga never feels alone again. This spirit becomes a counterpart, a "You," as it were, to whom she is devoted in love. It is no longer an abstract and one-dimensional intellectual spirit, but a fulfilling and inspiring relational spirit, Eros, that invites interaction and enables creative expression. Thanks to this inner connection to a real, albeit anonymous, counterpart and thanks to this knowledge gained through love, Olga was so fruitful for Eranos. She lived what Jung developed in his method of active imagination. In this method, he advised the imaginer to consider real what appears in the inner imagination, to relate to it, to appreciate it in love (for example by painting it) and to genuinely engage with it. *The Red Book* is testimony to this encounter with a spirit experienced as present, which became the basis for Jung's later creative insights. In the same way, Olga's attitude toward a living, present spirit honored in the stone became fruitful in the creative design of the Eranos gatherings. It was an artistic-imaginative attitude born of contemplation that she adopted rather than one of scientific discourse, an attitude that did better justice to the phenomenon of soul than artificial knowledge about the psyche. In short, she had a genuine encounter with the spirit of the place. Hence her wedding ring with the Greek words, *'H ágápe oúdépote píptei,* "Love never fails."

"Neumann" at Eranos

By John Hill

The person Neumann lived in one of the darkest moments of human history. He managed to get out of Germany just before the Nazis' attempt to exterminate his people. The figure of "Neumann" in the play *Eranos* embodies a struggle to maintain the relativity of opposites between good and evil and the masculine and feminine principles.

Through a confrontation with the Ape-man's single eye, which is also described as the single eye of the Godhead, Neumann is challenging unreflected, one-sided, dogmatic ethical assertions. The casuist Neumann expounds on this insight in his descriptions of the Nazis' brutal killings of women and children. He asks what is the greater evil: the killings of a single person or mass murder? Confronting an "Ape-man attitude," as witnessed in such horrific events, Neumann is appealing to the spectator, and to us all, to reflect on such questions so that we develop a more conscious and differentiated ethical attitude when confronting radical evil.

In the play, Neumann's ethical attitude becomes refined and developed in and through his conversations with Olga, the original founder of the Eranos conferences at Ascona. When Olga expounds on her personal experiences of the "Great Mother," Neumann is deeply moved and confesses that he is "in awe of the Great Mother." He believes the task of humanity is to integrate the Great Mother and not continue to split the masculine and feminine principles. He further elaborates on this transformation in citing the example of Job, who after his struggle with God, was redeemed and had three more daughters, giving them equal share in his inheritance, symbolizing a further enhancement of feminine values.

After elaborating the fundamental equality of men and women and explicitly rejecting a purely patriarchal definition of inheritance, Neumann resorts to developmental psychology. Here he professes to a reductive interpretation of heaven and hell, the former being experienced in the arms of a loving mother, the latter in bitter moments of abandonment.

In these short extracts, we see a radical movement from an extremely negative patriarchy, as witnessed in Nazi ideology and symbolized in the single-eyed Ape-man, to a celebration of "the Great Mother" that includes "a loving mother's embrace of her child." This movement appears to celebrate a transformation that had taken hold of Olga during her stay at Ascona. Olga's presence at the Eranos conferences left a profound impression on Neumann and helped him appreciate the feminine in new and creative ways.

The Eranos Play

By Gary Hayes

I was a bit perplexed when Murray asked me if I would like to play the part of Rabbi Baeck in the play that he and Henry Abramovitch had written about the Eranos Conference that took place after the war in 1947.

Eranos was a place that I knew about from the many commentaries that Jungians have written about it, but it was also a place that I had visited and spent a week at shortly after graduating from the Jung Institute in 1990. So, I do have a personal relationship with the magic and intrigue of the place.

On the other hand, I was not yet really familiar with the man Rabbi Baeck or with how he was involved with Jung and Eranos. I grew up in a very Protestant family, so it was a long time before I had any real notion about what rabbis are or how they function in the world. What I knew about Rabbi Baeck was that he was a renowned Jewish spiritual personality, and I was not sure whether I could do justice representing the scope of his powerful, charismatic being.

My first impulse was to decline Murray's interesting offer to play the Rabbi, mostly because I was not sure if I could do the job. Next, I started reading the script he sent me to learn more about the play and to look at the part that he wanted me to play. The more I read Baeck's lines, the more I became fascinated with the man and the part he plays in the piece. The more I became interested in the drama that was unfolding around him and his role in the play, especially his encounters with Jung, I started to realize that there were lines that he was speaking that moved me deeply; for instance when he says: "Evil occurs when individuals (I liked to say good people) remain silent." Or when he responds to Jung regarding his experience in the camps (Theresienstadt) with: "What that excruciating experience taught me most profoundly was to see each and every human individual as precious and unique." I started to realize how important these amazing words are, not just for me, but for all of us.

I find these lines poignantly relevant to our present time and the state of the world we are living in.

For me, many of Baeck's words speak directly to what is wrong with our mainstream politics and the way mainstream daily life is being conducted; namely, power first, or might makes right, and that together with an almost total lack of any spiritual values. The consequences of our adopting those ideologies are very clearly addressed in the play's Job scene and especially in Jung's *Answer to Job*. Either we are ignoring those lessons, or we are still blind to the archetypal structures that are driving those mainstream choices of how to conduct life in the world we now live in. Not only was Baeck acutely aware of the dangers of the trajectories modern life was moving toward, but he also talked about more conscious alternatives to the dangers of collective behaviors.

Back to my struggle with whether I should accept the offer to play Rabbi Baeck in the play.

I looked at the other people in the cast. The list included Paul Brutsche (Jung), John Hill (Erich Neumann), Dariane Pictet (Olga Fröbe-Kapteyn) and Kathrin Schaeppi (Aniela Jaffé).

Apart from Kathrin, I had seen all of these people on the stage in various other plays. To me, they are all experienced and talented actors. I, on the other hand, had no real acting experience. I asked myself, "How am I supposed to reach that level of stage performance that those people had clearly demonstrated?" However, when weighing in on how Rabbi Baeck's person intrigued me and the challenge of learning to interpret the Rabbi's role, I called Murray and told him that I had changed my mind and that I would accept his offer to play the Rabbi.

Immediately after I told Murray that, as well expected, fears and doubts about what I was getting myself into began to explode in me. But now I was committed to this scary adventure.

What then became quickly evident to me was that I would receive a great deal of support from Murray and Henry, and from everyone involved on the project. We started with discussions about the play and did some rehearsals online. The feedback after the rehearsals was always constructive and fair; we were all learning a lot about our characters and what the authors were trying to express about Eranos, the place and the interesting people who were returning there after the war to continue the project and the spirit of that project. But, and in addition to that, we were also openly discussing things that we were finding difficult about the script. I must say the authors were always open to our suggestions as to how to make the play better. This openness to our input I found very encouraging.

Early on Henry engaged a friend of his, Michael Posnick, a theater man from New York, to help coach us with the project. What an opportunity that was to have a person like Michael on board with his immense knowledge and experience. He taught us many important things that I had no idea about. One of the things I learned from him was that, of course, the words we are speaking are very important, but there are perhaps even more important things to learn about acting, for example, how to be on the stage and how to move. He taught us how to interact with the other players, how to look at them when they are speaking and how to genuinely listen to what they were saying.

After our dress rehearsal for our first performance at the Jungian Odyssey in Davos, I asked Michael about how actors keep their egos from getting in the way of what they are really supposed to be doing on the stage because that was what was happening to me. His response: You need to focus on what the other people up there on the stage with you are saying and doing and not on yourself.

Of course, I somehow knew this because it's what you need to do when you are working with your clients in analysis. You need to listen to the people you are working with, to listen and focus on everything they are saying and doing, not just the words. And, at the same time, you need to stay connected to yourself, not an easy thing to learn, but it's essential. This is one of the important things I learned from one of my supervisors, Mario Jacoby, when I was in training at the Jung Institute in Zurich.

It seems that I had forgotten this when I was trying to play Rabbi Baeck.

I was so glad, and it was such a relief for me when Michael, our beloved coach and instructor, pointed this out to me before our first performance.

After several online rehearsals and an actual dress rehearsal in Zürich with everyone present and Michael there online, we were seriously getting ready for our first live performance, which was scheduled for 2023 at the Jungian Odyssey in Davos. The audience there was made up of the Odyssey participants, the ISAP student participants and the dedicated Odyssey organizing committee. I must say we were treated very well in every respect, and the organizing committee did everything possible to support us with our premier performance.

Prior to the Davos event, I was not feeling very well. I was struggling with very low energy, so much so that it seemed to me that I had to drag myself around to get anything done. I had no idea what was wrong with me, I was scared, and I wasn't sure if I was up to the demands of performing, but I never once considered letting the others down at that point.

At a pre-performance dinner in Davos, Michael, our coach, revealed to us that he had just recovered from a very serious, life-threatening bout with illness. We were all very impressed with the amazing openness that Michael showed us. Sitting there at the restaurant table, I decided it was time for me to openly share that I felt I was going through something similar myself and that I was very concerned because, at that time, I had no idea about what was really ailing me. My sharing about that struggle was met with a wonderful response of genuine caring, empathy, and compassion. That was a huge gift to me.

Back in Zurich after the performance, I immediately contacted my doctors, who seemed to be very concerned about what these symptoms were all about. All kinds of tests were quickly arranged, and I spent the following days trying to cope with those unpleasant procedures and the anxiety around what was happening to me. What they discovered was that I had a drastically low iron deficiency. That turned out to be good news because it is, of course, something that can be treated, and the concerned suspicions of the doctors were met with relief from all sides.

The performance in Davos was a bit bumpy, but, all in all, it seemed to have been met with a good deal of positive feedback. There were some critiques, of course, but the people in the audience there for the most part liked and enjoyed the performance.

One of the things the audience mentioned was that they could have been given more context about Eranos, the place and its function. This helped us to understand and try to take it into account for further performances. I think all of us involved were very happy that it was so well received.

Our next goal was to try to get ready for performance number two in Zürich for the students, participants and colleagues at ISAP. To keep the momentum going, there were more online rehearsals. In addition, we were all invited to Dariane Pictet's lovely holiday home for more practice. The setting there could not have been better for what we were working on. The time spent at that amazing place was a very stimulating combination of intensive work on the play and relaxation in the wonderful small village near the famous resort of Gstaad. I felt things started to come together more and more there.

I think that had something to do with us getting to know each other better. This was especially important for me because Kathrin and I were new to acting and that group.

At Dariane's wonderful place, there were numerous discussions about the play. My impression that what we were doing was making more and more sense of "Eranos," the play, as we had this fortunate opportunity, with all present, to discuss what the play was about. This was also very helpful for me.

One of the things that became clearer through those discussions and the stimulating interactions around what we were doing with the material the authors had given us to work with, was that it gave us the opportunity to be able to become more familiar with the main themes of the play: Eranos the place, Eranos the history, especially the important role that Olga Fröbe-Kapteyn played in founding and creating the spirit of Eranos. But there was also more meaningful exchange about other pivotal themes, like the problem of evil as it was experienced during the Nazi regime and the havoc that reigned in Europe during and long after the war. One of the ways this was addressed in the play was through what the authors wrote about Baeck's encounter with Jung and the ensuing lines regarding the Book of Job.

Our next goal was to present the play in October to the students, analysts and other ISAP participants. I think it is generally known that presenting in front of one's peers and people one knows is somewhat a bit more of a challenge than when one doesn't know the people in the audience. The preparation for performance number two meant more rehearsals. One of them shortly before the actual performance involved on-site at the place where the play was being held, St. Anton's parish church in the center of Zurich. I'm not sure if everyone would agree, but if I remember correctly, that rehearsal did not go very smoothly; it seemed a bit bumpy to me, but I cannot explain why. Be that as it may, things were moving along toward our second show.

Then, on the night before the performance was scheduled, I was having dinner with Luis Moris, a young colleague who is very involved in what we were doing with the play. Among other things, he was making recordings of the sessions. He is also a filmmaker and, at some point, he was charged with thinking about the possibility of making some kind of film document of the Eranos play. In the middle of dinner that evening, I received an email from Murray, who told us that the play had been canceled because two of the main players, Dariane and John, had suddenly come down with the flu. To be honest, my first reaction was relief, thinking, "We don't have to do this tomorrow; maybe we have more time to get ready for the next performance." With a sigh of relief, I went home with the intention of getting a good night's sleep.

That feeling did not last very long because early the next morning, we received another email from Murray announcing to us that the play was on again. Apparently, the powers-that-be had contacted Murray, telling him that it was absolutely out of the question that we cancel. It seems the authors were told that we had to present something because a number of people had come from faraway places especially to see the play and that there was no disappointing them—the show must go on.

What happened was that Henry stayed up all night to produce a new, shorter version of the play, minus two very main players, Olga (Dariane) and Erich Neumann (John). The three of us left standing were asked to be there early the next day, the day of the performance, to rehearse the new shorter version. I was skeptical about how this all was supposed to work, but we, the ones left standing, were all there to do what we needed to do—make the play happen. Well, somehow most of the very loose ends began to fall into place. The more we addressed this new version, the more it started to flow for me, and I assume for Paul and Kathrin as well. I think it had a lot to do with Paul really pulling his part together. He was spectacular. I'm not sure, but I don't think the audience really noticed that we were presenting quite a different play from the original. I had the impression that the audience was happy with the play they were shown. Many of the people in the audience were people I know, and those who contacted me seemed to be very enthusiastic about the play and enjoyed it.

After the second performance of the play came the discussion and the debate about how to proceed with the Eranos project. There were several options. One was to make a film of the play.

Luis Moris, who is a filmmaker, proposed several ways we could make a film happen around the play. One of the things he proposed was an Eranos on-site version that could be done in summer 2024. After some discussion, we all decided that, due to the logistics and other factors, making a film document was probably too complicated. We just had to accept that making a film was too difficult and not practical. We then concluded that it was probably best to create a podcast. A tentative date was set, and we started moving in the direction of doing just that. It was decided that Luis would direct us using the assistance and facilities of his audio engineer friend and the friend's sound studio to make the audio version of the play.

So, now we had the opportunity with Luis' expertise and his friend's audio engineering experience and skills to create the play as a podcast.

For me, it was a very meaningful experience to be gently but firmly directed through the whole process of making that podcast. My sense was that we were doing this with the expert assistance of two very talented and experienced professionals. The responses to the podcast I have received so far all seem to confirm that.

I turn now to the final section of this commentary where I will talk about what was most meaningful and important to me about that experience.

The more I reflected about what we were doing with the material of the play, the more I became intrigued with Rabbi Baeck, the man, and the encounter that he had with Jung after the war and after his survival of his horrific experience of being one of the survivors of the concentration camps. It is beyond my comprehension to understand how anyone could survive such abuse. However, what I learned through my reading about the Rabbi is that like some very few and amazing others, he not only survived but he learned from that experience. For me this meant that I had much to learn from him and how he managed that.

The play also brings in the Book of Job and his encounter with the horrific, unfathomable, and unjustified abuse at the hands of Yahweh (God). This spurred me to return to what I knew about the Job narrative, and especially to return to Jung's *Answer to Job*, to reread that book and to address it anew with what I was learning from the play about Rabbi Baeck and about Baeck's encounter with Jung after the war.

From many of the various commentaries, we learn that Jung wrote *Answer to Job* late in his life. We know that the book was partially a reaction to his bout with a life-threatening illness where he experienced extreme suffering. We learn that he apparently wrote the piece in what people around him at the time referred to as a state of frenzy, working on it night and day and hardly paying attention to anything else until it was finished. I think we can say that he was gripped (*ergriffen*) by needing to create that document. And we learn that he had evidently commented that *Answer to Job* was the only piece he had ever written that he would in no way change or revise. From this I conclude that *Answer to Job* came out of a deep sense of suffering and immediacy for Jung. And more, I also conclude that there is a certain parallel between what Job experienced in his encounter with Yahweh in the Old Testament and with what Baeck experienced in the camps at the hands of his Nazi perpetrators. I also wonder if maybe Jung's motivation in writing *Answer to Job* had at least in part to do with his personal encounter with the Rabbi after the war.

The more I looked into the Job encounter, the more I began to recognize what Job accomplished through his unique and amazing demonstration of integrity in the face of how he was being unjustifiably abused by Yahweh. The play also touches on how Jung learned from his encounter with Baeck when they met in Zürich after the war and when they met again at Eranos before the opening of the Conference. I ask myself if this Rabbi Baeck that I am now learning more and more about could be considered a 20th-century version of Job. I will leave that up to the reader to ponder.

Finally, I would like to mention how glad I am that I reconsidered Murray's asking me to participate in the project, to thank him and Henry, the coauthors, and all of my fellow players who had to put up with me as a "newbie" as well as everybody else involved in the project for what they contributed to making the Eranos play a very meaningful experience.

Place, Period, Presence: Music for "Eranos"

By Barbara Helen Miller

In the following, I relate my journey in finding the appropriate music and then performing the short excerpts on the cello to 1) start the play, 2) provide mood between scenes, and 3) for the close of the play.

Making decisions on appropriate music is a team effort. For the first try out with the players, I had selected Vivaldi. Murray's feedback was that Vivaldi was too light; what was required was gravitas such as is found in Mahler. This led me to consider more the period in which the play "Eranos" was set. The mood of the period relates well with Gustave Mahler (1850–1911). Mahler was born to Jewish parents, was an Austro-Bohemian Romantic composer and acted as a bridge between the 19th century and the modernism of the early 20th century. All these elements are palpable in and for the figures in the play "Eranos."

Arnold Schoenberg (1874–1951) was an immediate musical successor to Mahler and so carried these elements further. My attention fell to *Verklärte Nacht* (*Transfigured Night*) Op. 4; string sextet in one movement composed by Schoenberg in 1899. The sextet was inspired by the poem of Richard Dehmel and by Schoenberg's strong feelings upon meeting his future wife.

Transfigured Night[15]

Two people walk through a bare, cold grove;
The moon races along with them, they look into it.
The moon races over tall oaks,
No cloud obscures the light from the sky,
Into which the black points of the boughs reach.
A woman's voice speaks:

I'm carrying a child, and not yours,
I walk in sin beside you.
I have committed a great offense against myself.
I no longer believed I could be happy
And yet I had a strong yearning
For something to fill my life, for the joys of
motherhood
And for duty; so I committed an effrontery,
So, shuddering, I allowed my sex
To be embraced by a strange man,
And, on top of that, I blessed myself for it.
Now life has taken its revenge:
Now I have met *you*, oh, you.

She walks with a clumsy gait,
She looks up; the moon is racing along.
Her dark gaze is drowned in light.
A man's voice speaks:

---

[15] Translated by Stanley Appelbaum.

May the child you conceived
Be no burden to your soul;
Just see how brightly the universe is gleaming!
There's a glow around everything;
You are floating with me on a cold ocean,
But a special warmth flickers
From you into me, from me into you.
It will transfigure the strange man's child.
You will bear the child for me, as if it were mine;
You have brought the glow into me,
You have made me like a child myself.

He grasps her around her ample hips.
Their breath kisses in the breeze.
Two people walk through the lofty, bright night.

The poem tells of an initial anxiety and feeling of failure that is transformed by companionship and love, that is, a transfigured night. This resonates with the story told by "Eranos." The poem, and hence the music, carry the story and mood of the play's figures: Olga Fröbe-Kaptyn's worries; Carl Gustav Jung's reassurances; Rabbi Leo Baeck's confrontations; Aniela Jaffé's thoughts; and Erich Neumann's participation.

The introduction music is from J.S. Bach's solo cello Suite V, Sarabande, and relates to the presence of the stone. The Narrator speaks: "A large Round Table stands under the trees in the garden there, and this is where the conversations in the play take place. To the left of the Table,

there is an impressive carved stone with the inscription, *Genio loci ignoto*—'to the unknown genius of this place.'"
My prompts to play chosen excerpts were:

1. Jung says about Neumann: "Upward and thunderous, like Chẻn, 'the Arousing.' When you meet him, you will see what I mean."
2. Olga on her daughter: "She was killed by the Nazis. Was I an evil mother?"
3. Jung: "nothing but *privatio boni*! .... It is like a pandemic driven by a wild and deadly virus."
4. Jung: "It has never left me. Called or not called, *It* is always present."
5. Neumann to Olga's invitation for next year's Eranos: "I feel as if I have finally found a home ... here at Eranos."
6. Rabbi Baeck to questions on the Book of Job: "We shall be like them, reborn from the dead."
7. Olga: "Heaven? Heaven is being home here with you All."
8. Narrator: "Eros! the Unknown Spirit of this place, Eranos."

The closing Schoenberg excerpt played by the cello is the actual closing bars of *Verklärte Nacht*. When looking into the appropriateness of *Verkärte Nacht* for the mood music between scenes, I suggested to the players to listen to the Hollywood String Quartet's recording on YouTube. This suggestion was for the most atmospheric performance and the performance that connects to my youth. Violinist/ conductor Felix Slatkin and his wife, cellist Eleanor Aller, led the string quartet. Their repertoire acted as a bridge between the 19th century and the modernism of the early 20th century. The Slatkin family were my teenage buddies. I followed them as I developed in Meerblome's youth orchestra, with rehearsals every Saturday in Plummer Park, Hollywood, and Fred Slatkin as principal cellist. Here again, Place, Period and Presence have formed/informed my experience.

Reflections on "Eranos, a Play"

By Dale Kushner

It is 1947, on the consecrated grounds of Eranos, near Ascona, Switzerland. The occasion is a ritual gathering of deep thinkers in the orbit of the renowned depth psychologist Carl Jung. Notably, most of the attendees—Eric Neumann, Aniela Jaffé, Rabbi Leo Baek, and the presiding maternal spirit of Eranos, Olga Frobe-Kaptyen—have survived the Nazi regime. Jung himself is in attendance, as are we, the audience. It is our great good fortune to be invited to participate as eavesdroppers to the unfolding conversations between the dramatis personae in this remarkable new play by Murray Stein and Henry Abramovitch.

More than 40 years earlier, Marie Rainer Rilke replied to a letter from an aspiring young poet offering the army cadet advice on poetic creation and life. The letters were later published as a book, *Letters to a Young Poet*. Rilke was no stranger to investigating interiority. Like his brothers and sisters at Eranos, he sought to distill meaning from the unfathomability of existence. In one of his most famous responses to the young Herr Kappus, he writes:

> Don't search for the answers, which could not
> be given to you now, because you would not
> be able to live them. And the point is, to live

everything. Live the questions now. Perhaps then, someday far in the future, you will gradually, without even noticing it, live your way into the answer.[16]

"Eranos," the play, is an enactment of the weighty questions circulating in the hearts and minds of those present at Eranos. Having witnessed the unspeakable, Jung and his companions endeavor to understand the nature of evil. What is evil? How does it spread? How can we comprehend evil if God is good? Is God good? Can we be forgiven for our passivity, our culpability, our dissociation from shadow aspects, personal and collective? How might self-interest deform our moral compass? In a time of chaos, what myths have been demolished? What new myths might restore us? Is the Great Mother a symbol or a majestic reality? Each question gestures toward other questions, and all of them are relevant to our postmodern lives. These are *our* questions, too.

The arresting magic of "Eranos," the play, is that its authors have humanized and embodied intellectual inquiry. What might have been a lifeless play of ideas is instead a drama about the search for meaning by palpably alive characters encountering a topsy-turvy world. In giving us a window into their search, we can hug their struggle close to our hearts and reflect on our own insecurities and dreams.

This seems to me the very best art can offer: a collaborative and generative exchange between the makers and receivers.

---

[16] R.M. Rilke, Letters to a Young Poet. Letter 4, July 16, 1903. Translated by Stephen Mitchell, Knopf Vintage, 1986.

At Eranos

By Michael Posnick

(By one who may have slept in the same bed once occupied by C.G. Jung.)

> *Now any of you who are for this road, prepare yourselves and put your feet on the Way.*
>
> Conference of the Birds
> Farid ud-din Attar

1.
come to the mountain
auditorium in the garden
the ensemble assembles
voicing voices of the dead
to quicken the living

waiting in the wings
the actors hover
between the passing
and the eternal,
a fragile fretwork
where listeners may look
into the unlimited.

surely, winds of wisdom and wonder
will rise from our roots
and flow through us
at Eranos

2.
across a pair of leather armchairs
across a liminal space
we have breathed in
so many sad and shadowed stories

they file by in dark frocks
bearing stone gods
snake goddesses
devouring spirits of the abyss
 faded photographs
 dreams and rings
 of lost promises
 and promised lands

now, round this table
these bones and breath shall live again

every once disembodied story
will burst and flow
through the porous membrane
to the listeners
to the starry skies
to the light
on the mountain

3.

notice how the room expands to silence
 when the master speaks.

her cello laces dreams
come jump with us
into the abyss

oh, the spirit of this place
oh, the spirit of this space.

The Daimon of Eranos

By Luis Moris

Writing about creativity toward the end of his life, Jung admitted that living with his ideas had been troubling for him. Throughout his life, Jung felt he had a daimon inside, "and in the end its presence proved decisive. It overpowered me, and if I was at times ruthless it was because I was in the grip of a daimon" (Jung, 1963/1996, p. 390). Jung had to create, he had no choice; he had to allow that daimon inside him to express itself, even if it meant suffering, to him and to others around him. I often wonder about Jung's daimon. Was it always there, or did it become more present and more powerful as he immersed himself in the unconscious psyche in midlife? For Jung, "The creative urge lives and grows in him like a tree in the earth from which it draws its nourishment" (Jung, 1922/2014b, para. 115).

When I first visited Eranos, I could not help feeling that the place has a spirit of some sort. This, I must say, is a rather unusual thing to me, especially in Europe—feeling the energy of a place is not something that occurs to me often. Only a few times this has happened to me in Switzerland. Another time was one night when I stayed for some time alone at the Psychology Club in Zurich—the club is haunted! Jung had an astonishing capacity to connect to places in this way. For instance, for Jung, Bollingen was "a place of spiritual connection" because he felt the land "is connected with the dead" (Jung, 1963/1995, p. 252-253). While traveling in a train in Mombasa, looking outside, Jung felt "a most intense *sentiment du déjà vu*" as he was "enchanted by the sight" (p. 283). He had the "feeling that I had already experienced this moment and had always known this world which was separated from me only by distance in time" (p. 283). Although Jung would have very much liked to visit the city of Rome, he decided not to go because he felt that he "was not really up to the impression the city would have made upon" him (p. 319). Eranos was no exception. Jung felt that Eranos has a spirit, and in fact asked for that spirit to be symbolized. The famous carved stone that says, *GENIO LOCI IGNOTO* ("To the Unknown Genius of the Place") is its representation. Not only do we humans have daimons, but places do, too.

As the producer and director of "Eranos," the podcast (which is found in the Blue Salamandra YouTube and Spotify channels), giving voice to the daimon of the place was of fundamental importance to me. My participation in the podcast began once the play had been written and the actors had rehearsed and acted several times. I was asked by Murray and Henry not to recreate a play for the theater. I had to create a podcast; an only-sound piece. So, my very first question I had for myself was how to represent the unknown genius of the place in sound. Important energy in the creation of the sound went into that question. We recorded "Eranos" with my good friend and professional sound technician, Joaquin Rivas, in his professional studio

El Cuartito, situated in the Third District of Zurich, a residential and at the same time bohemian district of the city. Recording the script for a podcast is a very different thing from rehearsing for a theater play. We recorded during an entire morning and the whole afternoon on a Saturday. In the afternoon, after lunch, once the actors had repeated their lines a few times and were tired of doing so, they allowed the spirit of the moment to take over. I could see how it was not their egos acting and trying to make it right, but how they got into their character, or rather, how their character got into them. The result of that day was that we recorded the authenticity of the moment. Days later, the creation and editing of the background sound, again, was intended to give Eranos, the land, the place it deserves— centrality. All the birds we hear in the podcast are from Ascona and its surroundings. The omnipresent sound of the water is the first and last thing heard in the podcast. The wind and the movement of the trees never stop.

You never know where a project with Murray and Henry is going to take you. Together we have created a movie[17] and three artistic podcasts.[18] I have been creating movies since 2009, first about tennis, now about Jungian psychology. Like many Jungians, I love movies and get a lot from them. Podcasts, on the other hand, were never

---

[17] *The Analyst and the Rabbi*, produced by Blue Salamandra (2002).
[18] *My Lunch with Thomas* (2023),
About friendship (2024),
Eranos (2024).
All podcasts are found in the Blue Salamandra YouTube channel and in most podcast platforms.

something I was particularly interested in, until Murray, Henry and I agreed to throw ourselves into the adventure of creating *My Lunch with Thomas,* our first podcast. In every project I have created with them something gets constellated. Energy controls what we do, and the result is always a surprise for everyone. As a producer, I never obtain what I first originally thought. Every project has its daimon, one might say.

I would like to end this brief reflection by mentioning how grateful I feel about having the possibility of immersing myself in these creative projects with teachers and friends that I love. Above all, I am in awe how they continue challenging themselves in new paths of creativity. Linking the idea of a daimon with the notion of vocation, Jung stated that the person who feels called "*must* obey his own law, as if it were a daemon whispering to him of new and wonderful paths. Anyone with a vocation hears the voice of the inner man: he is *called*" (Jung, 1934/2014b, para. 300). One could say that Murray, Henry, Paul, John, Kathrin, Darianne, and Gary feel called to create. Besides their work as analysts, they are always creating. It is through their concrete example that the individuation process becomes synonymous with allowing our creative daimon to appear in the world.

Luis Moris

Zurich, August 2024

Jung in the Garden of Eranos:
The Landscape of Analysis[19]

By Riccardo Bernardini

To write about Carl Gustav Jung's experience at Eranos is to show, first of all, how the theoretical *territories* explored in that crucial first two decades of the Conferences' life—from 1933 to 1952—were also the *boundaries* of a broader horizon in which Analytic Psychology, or Complex Psychology, was elaborated.[20] It means to document, moreover, how Jung's intellectual *itinerary* in Eranos—an ambitious "comparative study" of

[19] This writing, which originally appeared as "Jung nel giardino di Eranos: il paesaggio dell'analisi," *Eranos Yearbook*, 70 (2009-2010-2011): 731-38, reprinted (revised) in F. Vigna, eds., *L'Ombra del Flâneur. Scritti in onore di Augusto Romano* (Bergamo: Moretti&Vitali, 2014), pp. 35-46, is here revised and amplified in response to the play "Eranos" by Murray Stein and Henry Abramovitch.

[20] For a panoramic view of Eranos, see H.T. Hakl, *Der verborgene Geist von Eranos. Unbekannte Begegnungen von Wissenschaft und Esoterik. Eine alternative Geistesgeschichte des 20. Jahrhunderts* (Bretten: Scientia nova-Neue Wissenschaft, 2001), later revised and expanded as *Eranos. An Alternative Intellectual History of the Twentieth Century* (Montreal/Kingston: McGill-Queen's University Press, 2013). On Jung's involvement in the Eranos project, see more specifically R. Bernardini, *Jung a Eranos. Il progetto della psicologia complessa* (Milano: FrancoAngeli, 2011). For a list of Eranos Foundation publications over the years, see N. Cater and R. Bernardini, eds., *Spring: A Journal of Archetype and Culture, 92* (2015) [*Eranos. Its Magical Past and Alluring Future: The Spirit of a Wondrous Place*]. For a list of the Eranos *Yearbooks*, lecturers, and lecturers, see F. Merlini and R. Bernardini, eds., *Eranos in the Mirror: Views on a Moving Heritage. Eranos allo specchio: sguardi su una eredità in movimento* (Ascona: Aragno Eranos Ascona, 2019), and, constantly updated, the Eranos Foundation website: www.eranosfoundation.org.

the individuation process—was also a *journey* of discovery of the hermeneutic possibilities of this psychology. It means witnessing, finally, how the *traces* of the pioneering initiatives Jung promoted in conjunction with the Ascona summer symposia—an archive and an institute at Eranos for research on symbolism—were also the *steps* of a broader cultural rethinking that moved from such psychology. Yet, we know equally that identifying its *boundaries*, retracing its *path*, and reconstructing its *steps* would still not be sufficient to embrace, of Jung's involvement in Eranos, the entire *landscape*. That more intimate and discrete, but not for that reason marginal and secondary landscape, which precisely such boundaries, path, and steps complete, justify, and sustain.

Indeed, it is possible to recognize in the Jung of Eranos not only the constant "reference to clinical experience, from which he deduces the fundamental principles of theory,"[21] but also the "co-presence of culture and the red thread of analysis."[22] It is within the perimeter of the analytic dimension that Jung's intervention in Eranos can be restored, we believe, to its deepest sense. It is in a horizon of sessions, letters, dialogues, thoughts, images, visions, affections, separations, and reunions that it can be recovered in its densest background. It is beyond that threshold, which opens to "a boundless expanse full of

---

[21] A. Vitolo, "Le conferenze di Eranos," in A. Carotenuto, ed., *Trattato di Psicologia Analitica* (Torino: UTET, 1992), Vol. I, p. 660.
[22] A. Vitolo, Review of "Riccardo Bernardini, *Jung a Eranos. Il progetto della psicologia complessa*, FrancoAngeli, Milano 2012," *Rivista di Psicologia Analitica*, 84 (32, 2011): 270.

unprecedented uncertainty, with apparently no one inside and no one outside, no above and no below, no here and no there, no mine and no thine, no good and no bad. It is a world of water, where all life floats in suspension; where the realm of the sympathetic system, the soul of everything living, begins; where I am indivisibly this *and* that; where I experience the other in myself and the other-than-myself experiences me,"[23] that it can be reunited with its most authentic destiny. Jung's adherence to Eranos was not, in short, configured as an experience of exposition of theory alone, but rather as a passage in which, from analytic experience, theory and personal history took their cue and drew meaning.

Between Jung and Eranos founder Olga Fröbe-Kapteyn, it must be said, there was never a real analytic relationship.[24] At least initially, perhaps, she would have wished it, but it did not happen. In October 1934, having already had a few talks with Jung in Zurich, Olga Fröbe-Kapteyn had a vision in which she saw herself skating with him on the frozen surface of a lake. Holding hands, they performed movements together by drawing figures on the ice. They then walked around the perimeter of an immense rose that was beginning to grow three-dimensionally. As

[23] C.G. Jung, *Archetypes of the Collective Unconscious* (1934/1954), in *CW 9i*, p. 21.
[24] R. Ritsema, personal communication, August 20, 2003, Ascona-Moscia; see also W. McGuire, *Bollingen – An Adventure in Collecting the Past* (Princeton, NY: Bollingen Series, Princeton University Press, 1982), p. 26, and N. Neri, *Oltre l'Ombra. Donne intorno a Jung* (Roma: Borla, 1995), pp. 189 ff.; see also, more extensively, R. Bernardini, *op. cit.*, § 1.5, "Il rapporto tra Jung e Olga Fröbe-Kapteyn," pp. 83-112.

she and Jung stood at the center of this ice flower, the petals vanished, and only the outline at the base remained. This, too, at some point rose up and formed a small ice temple, the roof of which was an inverted rose with many petals. Jung and she, in the center of the temple, were holding hands. Jung was extremely impressed by Olga Fröbe-Kapteyn's account and by the fact that the two of them were together in a mandala[25]: From that moment, however, he did not want to work analytically with her anymore.[26]

Olga Fröbe-Kapteyn, in addition to conducting a lifelong self-analysis, consulted Erich Neumann and Léopold Szondi, the father of "destiny analysis" (*Schicksalsanalyse*) for analytical matters. Even in the absence of an analytic contract, she still continued to turn to Jung beyond matters concerning Eranos for advice on personal problems.[27] Jung suggested that she write down her dreams and try to interpret them, making himself available to meet her in person when she no longer knew how to deal with material from her unconscious.[28] The relationship with Jung represented a particularly fortunate experience for Olga Fröbe-Kapteyn, therefore, not only because her circle of acquaintances that stretched all over the world, and especially in the United

---

[25] Olga Fröbe-Kapteyn represented with a pictorial theme the Eranos mandala, the essence not only of her congressional project but also of her relationship with Jung. There are at least eight versions of this mandala, made between 1927 and 1949: see R. Bernardini, op. cit., pp. 100-06 and 165 ff.

[26] O. Fröbe-Kapteyn, "Die Eranos Mandala," undated typescript [1927-1949] (Eranos Foundation Archives, Ascona-Moscia), quoted in R. Bernardini, op. cit., p. 101; italics added.

[27] M. Anthony, *The Valkyries – The Women Around Jung* (Shaftesbury, Dorset: Element Books Limited, 1990), pp. 70 ff.

[28] H.T. Hakl, Der verborgene Geist von Eranos…, cit., p. 52, n. 87.

States, proved to be crucial for the financial survival of Eranos, but also and above all because Jungian psychology represented the "container" within which it was possible for her to deal with her own insights and questions of an inner nature.[29] It is Ximena de Angulo-Roell, since the 1950s Olga Fröbe-Kapteyn's personal assistant, who points to Jung's importance for Eranos precisely in having helped the latter to better understand her personal psychology and to give a broader meaning to what was happening to her inwardly.[30]

Although the correspondence between Jung and Olga Fröbe-Kapteyn does not record any significant disagreements, recalls Aniela Jaffé, it can be assumed that it was nonetheless not easy for two personalities as strong, independent, and creative as theirs to collaborate without coming into conflict or, at least, without finding themselves on divergent positions on certain issues. Although, on rare occasions, Jung even openly and severely expressed his disagreement, it was always for reasons of little consequence. And, in any case, never in the terms to which Olga Fröbe-Kapteyn resorted when speaking of their relationship[31] as a "battle."[32] However, in the last

---

[29] *Ibid.*, pp. 170 ff.

[30] X. de Angulo-Roelli, personal communications, August 17, 2010, Cavigliano, and March 31, 2012, Ascona.

[31] See A. Jaffé, "C.G. Jung und die Eranostagungen (Zum 100. Geburtstag von C.G. Jung)," *Eranos-Jahrbuch*, 44 (1975): 1-14; Engl. Ed., "C.G. Jung and the Eranos Conferences," *Spring* (1977): 201-12; It. Ed., "Carlo Gustav Jung e i convegni di Eranos," in Id., *Saggi sulla psicologia di Carl Gustav Jung* (Roma: Paoline, 1984), pp. 103-17 (pp. 115 ff.).

[32] O. Fröbe-Kapteyn, "Erster Abend...," undated typescript [prob. around 1957-1958], p. 1 (Eranos Foundation Archives, Ascona-Moscia), quoted in R. Bernardini, *op. cit.*, p. 106.

years of her life, through the practice of active imagination, Olga Fröbe-Kapteyn had the opportunity to process their enduring but conflicted relationship. The visions that were the outcome of that practice hint at a long and laborious confrontation with her own shadow[33]: "I am lying in bed," she wrote documenting that experience, "and I reflect on Jung and me, or rather, I see the *Eranos-landscape* of today and of before and the events that can still be seen quite clearly in this landscape. At this point the curtain opens and Jung enters. ... He is as I met him in the year 1935, so more than twenty years younger. He says, 'I am able to help you, especially since a clarification of our twenty-six-year relationship seems to me necessary. You might call it more a "battle" [*Kampf*] than a relationship, but you have now made it possible for me to take part in this mutual understanding [*Verständigung*], in that you were ready to have visions. It is the only way, this, because it leads through the *land of the sympathy of all things*. There everything is possible. Barriers are no longer present.'"[34]

Olga Fröbe-Kapteyn was able to recognize how the conflictual nature of their relationship was determined, in large part, by her projections. That is, the significance of their difficulties could be traced back to the intense negative transference toward Jung, onto whom, from 1934 to 1950, she had projected the image of a powerful and

[33] O. Fröbe-Kapteyn, "Der Schatten," typescript, May 17, 1957 (Eranos Foundation Archives, Ascona-Moscia), pp. 1 ff., quoted in *ibid.*, p. 90.
[34] O. Fröbe-Kapteyn, "Erster Abend...," cit., pp. 1 ff., quoted in *ibid.*, p. 107.

dark "Jahweh," as conveyed by the *Book of Job*.[35] It was this irrational and wrathful "Jahweh," for example, that Olga Fröbe-Kapteyn had encountered in the summer of 1948, when, upon her refusal to send the newly founded C.G. Jung-Institut the Eranos mailing list, Jung was seized by a sudden and severe attack of anger, in the face of which she was deeply disturbed and shaken.[36] Indeed, Olga Fröbe-Kapteyn continued, "Jung's appearance seems to change. Sometimes it is his face and benevolent expression. Sometimes his figure is huge, and then again he returns to his normal size. For an instant he appears demonic as in 1948, but immediately his features are human again, indeed more human than I have ever seen them. I see, as it were, the *Jahweh-projection* hovering over him, now entirely loosened, no longer firmly attached to him. ... The mighty image, demonic, unjust, greedy, full of power, indeed lethal, that I had built for myself of Jung and that extended the taboo-Jahweh's law, precisely on Eranos, has now become defenseless. The old law has dissolved, and I find myself under a new law. So from Jung detaches, and falls, much unreal guilt."[37]

After more than 15 years of "battle," the Jahwistic image projected onto Jung finally crumbled, giving way to the image of Jung as an individual. Olga Fröbe-Kapteyn

---

[35] O. Fröbe-Kapteyn, *op. cit.*, p. 23, quoted in *ibid.*
[36] O. Fröbe-Kapteyn, *op. cit.*, p. 19; and C. Ritsema-Gris, "L'Œuvre d'Eranos et Vie d'Olga Froebe-Kapteyn," undated, typescript (Eranos Foundation Archives, Ascona-Moscia), p. 23.
[37] O. Fröbe-Kapteyn, *op. cit.*, pp. 1 f., quoted in R. Bernardini, *op. cit.*, pp. 107 ff.

recognized how behind this projection lay her own negative animus,[38] namely, her aggressive masculine side. This projection, although destructive, had nevertheless helped her to confront her own masculine side, namely that animus which, in its positive aspect, had enabled her to give birth to Eranos. Olga Fröbe-Kapteyn reflected again, "If I had not projected 'Jahweh' I would not have come to grips with this archetype, I would not even have attempted it, because I would not have arrived at the problem. I would never have understood to the end that it was in myself. ... Jung, now, has become 'human,' since I no longer deify him through projection-Jahweh. His human stimuli are no longer altered through the speaker of Jahweh, oversized and crammed with archetypal energy and violence. Perhaps, now, the real confrontation can take place. As my resentments and condemnations have disappeared, something has been transformed in me, and certainly in Jung, and this transformation embraces the concept of freedom for both of us, for neither obsession nor projection is freedom, but always constraint and contraction."[39]

The acceptance and integration of this hitherto split and projected part of the self meant that, from the point of view of their relationship, what had hitherto been a "battle" gradually changed into a "tender and reconciling

---

[38] On the idea of negative animus, see, in particular, C.G. Jung, *Visions. Notes from the Seminar Given in 1930-1934*, ed. C. Douglas (London/New York, NY: Routledge, 1998), vol. I, pp. 560, 614 and 622.
[39] O. Fröbe-Kapteyn, "Erster Abend...," cit., pp. 2 ff., quoted in R. Bernardini, *op. cit.*, pp. 108 ff.

feeling without affection: a kind of compassion."[40] At the conclusion of the experience, Olga Fröbe-Kapteyn received this message from Jung, who appeared in her vision: "It is time. I think we have done it. And now, you write the story of Eranos, because for the first time you see him without taboos, and you are free. Maybe we will see each other again, maybe not, but peace is in us."[41]

The epistolary exchange between Jung and Olga Fröbe-Kapteyn, which began in the early 1930s and is still only minimally included in the *corpus* of Jung's letters, continued until his passing. The missives of the last 10 years, in particular, are the visible sign of an intimate bond, never broken, and the expression of Jung's sincere gratitude to Olga Fröbe-Kapteyn and her creation, Eranos, on the one hand, and to Olga Fröbe-Kapteyn toward Jung, on the other hand, for the support given to her not only on the organizational level for Eranos, but perhaps even more so on the personal level, in her continuous confrontation with her own interiority: a confrontation that, from the second half of the 1920s to the mid-1930s also found expression in pictorial form, the so-called *"Blue Book,"* which Eranos Foundation is currently studying, composing, and gradually bringing to publication.[42]

---

[40] O. Fröbe-Kapteyn, *op. cit.*, p. 3, quoted in *ibid.*, p. 109.

[41] O. Fröbe-Kapteyn, *op. cit.*, pp. 21 ff., quoted in *ibid.*, p. 110. The work referred to by Olga Fröbe-Kapteyn is probably *Die Geschichte von Eranos*, a recount of reflections dated between 1952 and 1958 which, in the author's plan, would have been intended to lead to the writing of a "history of Eranos" from the point of view of its inner life: see R. Bernardini, *op. cit.*, pp. 19 and 110, fn. 429.

[42] A list of publications to date on Olga Fröbe-Kapteyn's art is available in R. Bernardini and R. Merlini, "The *Blue Book* of Olga Fröbe-Kapteyn, Founder of

In August 1951, for example, on the occasion of Olga Fröbe-Kapteyn's 70th birthday, Jung wrote this message, which in some ways summarized the role played by Eranos in the construction of Analytical Psychology: "Eranos, thanks to Mrs. Fröbe's resourcefulness and devotion, has become an institution to which one can wish a long future, which represents in Europe the only occasion where, beyond all specialist limitations, experts and laymen animated by spiritual interests can come together to exchange their views. Eranos anticipated by twenty years today's efforts toward the reunification [*Zusammenfassung*] of all the sciences and thus made a contribution in its own unique way to European intellectual history. This success would not have been possible, however, had it not found in Dr. [Daniel] Brody a publisher as sensitive as he was devoted to the cause, who was not afraid to take on the risk of the voluminous annals [of the *Eranos-Jahrbücher*]. What made Eranos so valuable to me personally was the fact that Mrs. Fröbe's hospitable home offered from time to time the opportunity for informal discussions around the Round Table. I remember with pleasure and gratitude the countless evenings that were so rich in stimulation and teaching and that provided me with just what I needed so much, namely personal empathic contact [*Fühlungnahme*]

Eranos," in R. Gygax, eds., *Olga Fröbe-Kapteyn. Artista – ricercatrice. Volume pubblicato in occasione della mostra Olga Fröbe-Kapteyn: artista-ricercatrice, Museo Casa Rusca, Locarno, 8 agosto 2024-12 gennaio 2025* (Locarno/Ascona/ Bellinzona: Museo Casa Rusca/Fondazione Eranos/Casagrande, in collaboration with Kunsthalle Mainz, 2024), pp. 44-51.

with other fields of knowledge. For this I owe Mrs. Fröbe the deepest thanks."[43]

In a letter dated June 2, 1956, he wrote to her: "Dear Mrs. Fröbe, I thank you wholeheartedly for sending me, and so amicably dedicating to me, the XXIV volume of the *Eranos-Jahrbücher* on the subject 'Man and the Sympathy of All Things,' and likewise for your note. Even a first glance promised an interesting read; I only regret that I must postpone it until my summer vacation period; overwork deprives me at the moment of the necessary quiet. Eranos conferences have always offered me an abundance of remarkable intellectual stimulation, and the exchange of thoughts with people of similar interests as well as the resonance of a prepared audience have been a beautiful and important experience for me. Unfortunately, age now prevents me from attending symposia: my strengths would not quite be able to stand up to the inevitable onslaught of all those people. Now more than ever, I need peace of mind and must carefully avoid all meetings with lots of people. Even more so, therefore, the *Jahrbücher* are now something precious to me, since they communicate to me the spiritual essence of the meetings, although I must call to mind, alone, the sunlight, the lake and old friends. For this year's conference I wish you a good and fruitful outcome, and

---

[43] C.G. Jung, "Dank an Frau Froebe," August 1951, typescript (Eranos Foundation Archives, Ascona-Moscia), merged in L. Heyer-Grote, ed., "Gratulationen zum 70. Geburtstag Olga Froebe-Kapteyn am 19 Oktober 1951," 1951, collection of manuscripts and typescripts (Eranos Foundation Archives, Ascona-Moscia), and quoted (in part) in A. Jaffé, *op. cit.*, p. 106 and (in full) in R. Bernardini, *op. cit.*, pp. 77 ff. English translation by the author.

I would be grateful if you could convey this wish to the individual speakers. Yours sincerely, C.G. Jung."[44]

On March 30, 1957, in a note prepared for a publication celebrating the first 25 years of the life of Eranos, Jung wished, "May the light of the European spirit, which in this time of darkness has come out of Eranos for so many years, still have as a gift a long life, so that it may fulfill its role as a beacon of a European union."[45]

In his old age, recalls Aniela Jaffé, epistolary advice and explanations greatly wearied Jung, who therefore generally refused to give any. For Olga Fröbe-Kapteyn, however, he did not hesitate to make an exception. Especially late in life, what weighed heavily on Olga Fröbe-Kapteyn was the loneliness into which she was abruptly catapulted as guests left Eranos after the lively symposium period; she was therefore very grateful to those few who could extend their stay in Ascona-Moscia by a few days.[46] During the long winters, epistolary exchanges were probably therefore particularly important to her.

In 1960, following a serious operation on her eyes, she was forced to wear a black bandage for eight days. As Mircea Eliade recounts in his diary, Olga Fröbe-Kapteyn was distressed by the constant darkness and could not

---

[44] C.G. Jung, letter to O. Fröbe-Kapteyn, June 2, 1956 (University Archives, ETH-Bibliothek, Zürich; © Foundation of the Works of C.G. Jung), quoted in R. Bernardini, *op. cit.*, pp. 110 f.; English translation by the author.
[45] Quoted in O. Fröbe-Kapteyn, ed., *25 Jahre Eranos. 1933-1957* (Zürich: Rhein-Verlag, 1957), page not numbered [p. 5]; English translation by the author.
[46] C. Ritsema-Gris, *op. cit.*, p. 32; English translation by the author.

remain alone for a moment without finding comfort in the nurse's hand. However, her momentary blindness stimulated a series of visions which, dictated to her secretary, she had delivered to Jung on June 24, 1960. In the first vision, there was a ruined cathedral, at night. She saw herself on scaffolding, very high up, near the dome and, at a certain moment, realized that the cathedral was herself. So she knelt down, waiting to be pierced in the back by a spear.[47] Jung wrote her back a few days later, saying that the surgical operation had a psychic parallel: Just as the threat of cataracts, and thus blindness, was an equivalent of the danger of sinking into the unconscious, of spiritual death, so her operation was equivalent to a new birth, and the recovery of the visual faculties to the salvation of conscious life from the engulfment of the unconscious.[48] This was the last letter Jung wrote to her.[49]

The words with which Olga Fröbe-Kapteyn concluded one of her last missives to Jung turn out to be understandable: "During the experiences of the last weeks [of hospitalization], I always held on to some expression

---

[47] O. Fröbe-Kapteyn, letter to C.G. Jung, June 24, 1960 (University Archives, ETH-Bibliothek, Zürich; © Foundation of the Works of C.G. Jung / Eranos Foundation Archives, Ascona-Moscia), quoted in R. Bernardini, *op. cit.*, p. 111; see also M. Eliade, *Fragments d'un journal I-III, 1945-1985* (Paris: Gallimard, 1973-1991); It. Ed., *Giornale* (Torino: Boringhieri, 1976), p. 255.

[48] C.G. Jung, letter to O. Fröbe-Kapteyn, June 28, 1960 (University Archives, ETH-Bibliothek, Zürich; © Foundation of the Works of C.G. Jung / Eranos Foundation Archives, Ascona-Moscia), quoted in R. Bernardini, *op. cit.*, p. 111.

[49] A subsequent missive to Olga Fröbe-Kapteyn from Jung was written by Aniela Jaffé on September 15, 1960 (Eranos Foundation Archives, Ascona-Moscia); see R. Bernardini, *op. cit.*, p. 111.

of his or a sentence from the *I Ching*, and thus I was able to realize what a blessing his cooperation was for Eranos and for me personally. Despite many personal difficulties, I always stuck to what She said. And now, after twenty-seven years, more than ever. I am deeply happy to have the opportunity to tell you."[50]

Jung's journey through Eranos is ultimately inseparable from that landscape which, on closer inspection, we might recognize as a *garden:* that of a ceaseless, inner work that, from the very beginning, has supported, founded, and guided the cultural and scientific dimension of the conferences: A garden destined for the cultivation of that "knowledge of the heart [which] is in no book and is not to be found in the mouth of any teacher but grows out of you like the green seed from the dark earth" and which—it is Jung again who tells us—"you can attain … only by living your life to the full." It is the garden of a knowledge that comes from life, and that speaks of life, to the cultivation of which Jung and Olga Fröbe-Kapteyn contributed as to a "lifework, [which] is like a ship that one has built and equipped oneself, launched down the ramp and entrusted to the sea, steered towards a distant goal and then left like a passenger, in order to sit on the shore and gaze after it till it is out of sight. Like all three-dimensional things it gradually sinks below the horizon. What remains is what has been."

---

[50] O. Fröbe-Kapteyn, letter to C.G. Jung, June 24, 1960, cit.; also quoted in A Jaffé, *op. cit.*, p. 117, and in R. Bernardini, *op. cit.*, pp. 111 f.

References

Abramovitch, Henry (Ed.) (2006). *Special Thematic Issue: On Erich Neumann. Harvest: International Journal for Jungian Studies* 52 (2): 1-199.

Baeck, Leo (1955/1964). *This People Israel: The Meaning of Jewish Existence.* Translated by Albert H. Friedlander. London: W.H. Allen.

Bernardini, Riccardo (2011). *Jung a Eranos: Il Progetto della psicologia complessa.* Milan: Franco Angeli.

_____. (2016). "Neumann at Eranos." *Turbulent Times, Creative Minds: Erich Neumann and C.G. Jung in Relationship (1933-1960),* edited by Erel Shalit and Murray Stein. Asheville, NC: Chiron Publications.

Bernardini, Riccardo & Bellini, Fabio (2021) Olga Fröbe-Kapteyn (1881–1962): Through images at the Origins of the Eranos Conferences. https://aras.org/articles/olga-fröbe-kapteyn-1881–1962-woman's-individuation-process-through-images-origins-eranos.

Cunningham, Adrian (2007). "Victor White, a Memoir." A. Lammers & A. Cunningham (eds.), *The Jung-White Letters.* London and New York: Routledge.

Eliade, Mircea (1958). *The Sacred and the Profane,* New York: Harcourt, Brace and World.

Ferrara, Marianna (2021). *Olga Fröbe-Kapteyn's Ashram: The Great Mother and the Personal History of Eastern Religions.* ASDIWA: Revue Genevoise d'Anthropologie et d'Histoire des Religions, vol. 16, 79-94.

Fischli, Elena (2023). "Historical Commentary." In A. Jaffé, *Reflections on the Life and Dreams of C..G. Jung.* Einsiedeln, Switzerland: Daimon Verlag.

Fröbe-Kapteyn, Olga (1933–1954). *Eranos Jahrbuch vols. 1–20.* Zurich: Rhein-Verlag.

Gygax, Raphael (2024). "Olga Fröbe-Kapteyn's Artistic Research: The Eranos Archive for Research in Symbolism." *Olga Fröbe-Kapteyn Artista-Ricercatrice.* Museo Casa Rusca: Fondazione Eranos, pp. 82-87.

Hakl, Hans Thomas (2013). *Eranos: An Alternative Intellectual History of the Twentieth Century.* Translated by Christopher McIntosh. Sheffield, UK: Equinox.

Hillman, J. (1970). "The Language of Psychology and the Speech of Soul." *Eranos-Jahrbuch* XXXVII/1968, Rhein-Verlag: Zürich.

Jaffé, Aniela (1966/1971). *The Myth of Meaning.* Translated by R.F.C. Hull. New York: G.P. Putnam's Sons.

_____. (2023). *Reflections on the Life and Dreams of C.G. Jung.* Einsiedeln: Daimon Verlag.

Jung, C.G. (1952/1969). *Answer to Job. Collected Works,* vol. 11. Princeton, NJ: Princeton University Press.

_____. (1961) *Memories, Dreams, Reflections.* Recorded and edited by A. Jaffé. New York: Random House.

_____. (1963/1995). *Memories, Dreams, Reflections.* Fontana Press: London

_____. (2014a). The Development of the Personality. In H. Read et al. (Eds.), *The Collected Works of C. G. Jung: Vol. 17. The Development of the Personality.* London: Routledge & Kegan Paul. (Originally published in 1934)

_____. (2014b). On the Relation of Analytical Psychology to Poetry. In H. Read et al. (Eds.), *The Collected Works of C. G. Jung: Vol. 15. The Spirit in Man, Art, and Literature.* London: Routledge and Kegan Paul. (Originally published in 1922)

Knox, Oliver, (2021). *The Buddha at Eranos, Journal of Global Buddhism, Vol.22* (1): 1–17.

Lammers, Ann & Adrian Cunningham (Eds.) (2007). *The Jung-White Letters.* London and New York: Routledge.

Liebscher, Martin (Ed.) (2015). *Analytical Psychology in Exile: The Correspondence of C.G. Jung & Erich Neumann.* Princeton, NJ: Princeton University Press.

McGuire, William (1982). *Bollingen. An Adventure in Collecting the Past.* Princeton, NJ: Princeton University Press.

Neumann, Erich (1948/1969). *Depth Psychology and a New Ethic.* Translated by Eugene Rolfe. New York: G.P. Putnam's Sons.

_____. (1954/1963). *The Great Mother. An Analysis of the Archetype.* Translated by Ralph Manheim. Princeton, NJ: Princeton University Press.

Scholem, Gerschom (1979). "Identifizierung und Distanz: ein Rückblick." *Eranos Jahrbuch* 48

Sorge, Giovanni (2012). "Love as Devotion: Olga Fröbe-Kapteyn's Relationship with Eranos and Jungian Psychology." University of Zurich. https://www.zora.uzh.ch/id/eprint/74881/1/sorge_eranos_2012.pdf

Stein, Murray (2016). "Erich Neumann and C.G. Jung on 'The Problem of Evil.'" *Turbulent Times, Creative Minds: Erich Neumann and C.G. Jung in Relationship (1933-1960)*, edited by Erel Shalit and Murray Stein. Asheville, NC: Chiron Publications.

Tevebring, Frederika (2023). *Images from the Collective Unconscious-Olga Fröbe-Kapteyn and the Eranos Archive.* https://publicdomainreview.org/essay/images-from-the-collective-unconscious/.

White, V. (1952/1961). *God and the Unconscious.* Cleveland and New York: Meridian Books.

Zimmer, Heinrich. (1984). *Artistic Form and Yoga in the Sacred Images of India*, Princeton, NJ: Princeton University Press.

Author Bios

Henry Abramovitch, Ph.D., is the founding President of Israel Institute of Jungian Analysis in honor of Erich Neumann. He is Professor Emeritus, Tel Aviv University, the author of *Brothers & Sisters: Myth & Reality, Why Odysseus Came Home as a Stranger*, a detective story, *Panic Attacks in Pistachio*, among others. With Murray Stein, he has coauthored a series of plays, including *The Analyst and the Rabbi, Speaking of Friendship*, and *Eranos*. He lives and practices in Jerusalem.

Riccardo Bernardini, Ph.D., Psy.D., serves as Scientific Secretary of the Eranos Foundation (Ascona, Switzerland). He is the Founding President of the Institute of Analytical Psychology and Psychotherapy (IPAP), Postgraduate School of Psychotherapy (Ivrea, Italy). He is a member of the Associazione per la Ricerca in Psicologia Analitica (ARPA, Italy) and the International Association for Analytical Psychology (IAAP). Since 2019, he also has served as Secretary of the Order of Psychologists of Piedmont (Italy). He is Adjunct Professor of Psychology of Evil and Radicalization Processes at Turin University (Italy). His books include *Jung a Eranos. Il progetto della psicologia complessa* (2011) and *Rebirth symbols in the Basilica of San Miniato al Monte in Florence, From Joachim of Fiore to C.G. Jung* (2022). He has led the publication C.G. Jung's *The Solar Myths and Opicinus de Canistris. Notes of the Seminar*

Given at Eranos in 1943 (edited with G.P. Quaglino and A. Romano, 2014–2015) and the original edition of Jung's *Rebirth. Text and Notes of the Lecture held at Eranos in 1939* (edited with F. Merlini, 2020).

Paul Brutsche, Ph.D., studied philosophy and theology in Fribourg, Paris, and Innsbruck, psychology at the University of Zurich, and got a diploma in Analytical Psychology at the C.G. Jung-Institute Zürich. He has practiced since 1975 as a Jungian therapist in Zurich. He is training analyst, supervisor and lecturer at The International School of Analytical Psychology Zurich (ISAP Zurich). He has been President of the former Swiss Society of Analytical Psychology SGAP, the C.G. Jung-Institute Zürich and ISAP Zurich. He has given seminars and lectures in Switzerland and abroad and writes mainly on picture interpretation, symbolism in art, and questions of creativity.

Gary R. Hayes, lic. phil., (University of Zurich) and Swiss Federally licensed Psychotherapist. Former Training Analyst and Supervisor at C.G. Jung Institute Küsnacht. Currently Training Analyst, Supervisor, lecturer and seminar leader at ISAP Zurich. In private practice in Zurich since 1990.

John Hill, M.A., is a Training and Supervising Analyst at ISAP Zurich. He has lectured internationally and been the IAAP Liaison person for the Developing Group in Georgia for many years. He was the first Zurich Lecture Series author/speaker in 2009, and his book is titled *At Home in the World.* He has played many roles with the ISAP Ensemble, including Father Victor White in *The Jung-White Letters,*

Rabbi Leo Baeck in *The Analyst and the Rabbi*, and Elijah, Isdubar, and Philemon in "Scenes from *The Red Book*." His area of special interest has been using psychodrama with dreams and fairy tales.

Dale M. Kushner is a novelist, poet, and essayist. Her debut novel, *The Conditions of Love*, published by Grand Central, was nominated for the Texas Library Association Award for Outstanding Adult Fiction. Her poetry collection *M* was honored by Special Mention in the Pushcart Prize 2024. Kushner's widely regarded writings have appeared in *Strange Attractors: Lives Changed by Chance*, University of Massachusetts Press, *Jung's Red Book for Our Time: Searching for Soul Under Postmodern Conditions, Volume 4*, Chiron Publications, *Jewish Currents*, and elsewhere. *Transcending the Past*, her popular monthly online column for *Psychology Today* is informed by her study of Jungian psychology. She has recently been filmed for a documentary on dreams now in production called *Between Two Worlds*. She has just completed her second novel.

Barbara Helen Miller, Ph.D., is a psychoanalyst (C.G. Jung) in private practice, member of International Association for Analytical Psychology, Training Analyst for the IAAP program in Tbilisi Georgia; anthropologist in cooperation with Research Group Circumpolar Cultures, her research a case study on Sámi healers in Porsanger, Norway. Many of her publications attempt to bring Analytical Psychology and shamanism into fruitful dialogue.

Luis Moris, MA, is a Jungian analyst and lecturer at the International School of Analytical Psychology (ISAP Zurich). He is the editor of *Confronting Death* (Chiron Publications, 2024) and *A Jungian Legacy, Tom Kirsch* (Chiron Publications, 2019). He is the founder of Blue Salamandra. Luis lives and has a private practice in Zurich.

Dariane Pictet has a degree in Comparative Religion from Columbia University and is a Diplomate of the C.G. Jung Institute, Zurich. She also has an Advanced Diploma in Existential Psychotherapy from Regent's University, London, where she was a Visiting Lecturer for several years. She is a training and supervising analyst at ISAP-ZURICH and GAP in London, and she lectures internationally. She enjoys poetry and theater. Her latest publications are "Movements of Soul in *The Red Book*," in *Jung's Red Book for Our Time*, vol. 1. ed. Murray Stein and Thomas Arzt (Chiron, 2017), and "Mirroring Self Love" in Quandrant, vol. 19 (2021).

Michael Posnick is an American director and teacher of theater. His productions have been seen at the Manhattan Theatre Club, New York Philharmonic and Yale Repertory Theatre. His most recent work includes *Pharaoh,* a retelling of the Exodus myth in Kathakali style by Misha Shulman, and *Eranos* by Murray Stein and Henry Abramovitch for the Jungian Odyssey in Davos, Switzerland. He is Professor Emeritus of Manhattanville University and has taught at Yale, Hunter College, the National Theatre Institute, and for 25 years worked with the National Theatre of the Deaf.

He coproduced the inaugural performances of *HATUEY, MEMORY OF FIRE*, a Cuban-Yiddish nightclub opera by Frank London, in Havana, Cuba;, and coauthored *Nine Contemporary Jewish Plays*. Posnick holds degrees from Yeshiva University and the Yale School of Drama.

Kathrin U. Schaeppi, MS, MLA, MFA, is a federally licensed Jungian Depth Psychologist and Psychotherapist, Training Analyst and Supervisor. She regularly teaches and gives seminars locally and internationally. At ISAP Zurich she heads the Picture Interpretation Department, is cofounder of its Picture Collection, and is a member of the Zürich Lecture Series team. Her walking guide *C.G. Jung: The Basel Years* is planned for publication in Fall 2025. (www.kschaeppi.ch)

Murray Stein, Ph.D. is a Training and Supervising Analyst at the International School of Analytical Psychology Zurich (ISAP-ZURICH). He has been president of the Chicago Society of Jungian Analysts (1980-1985), the International Association for Analytical Psychology (2001–2004) and of ISAP Zurich (2008–2012). He lectures internationally and is the author of *Jung's Map of the Soul, Outside Inside and All Around, The Mystery of Transformation* and many other books and articles. Nine volumes of his *Collected Writings* have been published to date. He lives in Switzerland and has a private practice in Zurich and from his home in Goldiwil, Switzerland.

www.ingramcontent.com/pod-product-compliance
Lightning Source LLC
Chambersburg PA
CBHW020246290326
41930CB00038B/415